MW00454389

Texas Legal Research

CAROLINA ACADEMIC PRESS
LEGAL RESEARCH SERIES

Suzanne E. Rowe, Series Editor

Arizona — Tamara S. Herrera

Arkansas — Coleen M. Barger

California — Hether C. Macfarlane & Suzanne E. Rowe

Colorado — Robert Michael Linz

Connecticut — Jessica G. Hynes

Federal — Mary Garvey Algero, Spencer L. Simons, Suzanne E. Rowe,
Scott Childs & Sarah E. Ricks

Florida, Third Edition — Barbara J. Busharis & Suzanne E. Rowe

Georgia — Nancy P. Johnson, Elizabeth G. Adelman & Nancy J. Adams

Idaho — Tenielle Fordyce-Ruff & Suzanne E. Rowe

Illinois, Second Edition — Mark E. Wojcik

Iowa — John D. Edwards, M. Sara Lowe, Karen L. Wallace
& Melissa H. Weresh

Kansas — Joseph A. Custer & Christopher L. Steadham

Louisiana — Mary Garvey Algero

Massachusetts — E. Joan Blum

Michigan, Second Edition — Pamela Lysaght & Cristina D. Lockwood

Minnesota — Suzanne Thorpe

Missouri, Second Edition — Wanda M. Temm & Julie M. Cheslik

New York, Second Edition — Elizabeth G. Adelman, Theodora Belniak
& Suzanne E. Rowe

North Carolina — Scott Childs

Ohio — Katherine L. Hall & Sara Sampson

Oregon, Second Edition — Suzanne E. Rowe

Pennsylvania — Barbara J. Busharis & Bonny L. Tavares

Tennessee — Sibyl Marshall & Carol McCrehan Parker

Texas — Spencer L. Simons

Washington, Second Edition — Julie Heintz-Cho, Tom Cobb
& Mary A. Hotchkiss

Wisconsin — Patricia Cervenka & Leslie Behroozi

Texas Legal Research

Revised Printing

Spencer L. Simons

Suzanne E. Rowe, Series Editor

CAROLINA ACADEMIC PRESS

Durham, North Carolina

Library of Congress Cataloging-in-Publication Data

Simons, Spencer L.
Texas legal research / Spencer L. Simons.
    p. cm. -- (Carolina Academic Press legal research series)
Includes bibliographical references and index.
ISBN 978-1-61163-195-1 (alk. paper)
1. Legal research--Texas. I. Title. II. Series.

KFT1275.S56 2009
340.072'0764--dc2222   2009004948

Carolina Academic Press
700 Kent Street
Durham, North Carolina 27701
Telephone (919) 489-7486
Fax (919) 493-5668
www.cap-press.com

Printed in the United States of America.

To Alexandra,
for her support, encouragement, and patience

Summary of Contents

Contents

List of Tables and Figures

Tables

Figures

Series Note

The Legal Research Series published by Carolina Academic Press includes an increasing number of titles from states around the country. The goal of each book is to provide law students, practitioners, paralegals, college students, laypeople, and librarians with the essential elements of legal research in each state. Unlike more bibliographic texts, the Legal Research Series books seek to explain concisely both the sources of state law research and the process for conducting legal research effectively.

Preface and Acknowledgments

The primary audience for *Texas Legal Research* is law students in first-year legal research and writing programs or in advanced legal research classes where the specifics of Texas legal research are studied. The book is also useful to lawyers, paralegals, college students, laypersons, and anybody needing a handbook on how to find and use Texas legal resources.

In the three years since the publication of *Texas Legal Research*, changes have accumulated in resources cited in the text and the locations at which they can be found. This revised printing of *Texas Legal Research* includes updates regarding the Texas codification project, revised Texas Supreme Court rules regarding unpublished opinions, changed citation rules under the eighteenth edition of the *The Greenbook: Texas Rules of Form*, and updated information about online legal information sources. All citations to online and print sources and information have been brought up to date.

The book serves a dual purpose. It is first of all an instructional text. Law students must develop an understanding of the relationships of legal authority to the legal system, legal analysis, and the practice of law. Students must also master the practical skills of finding relevant authority. Most law students are preparing for a career in which most of their research will be conducted in the law of their state. This book uses Texas legal resources to introduce basic concepts of legal analysis and practice, teach the skills of legal research, and acquaint students with the particular legal authority found in Texas. Corresponding federal resources are discussed for each type of legal authority. Research in the law of other states is discussed as needed to provide context or where Texas practice differs from the general practice in other states.

The book may also be used as a field guide to Texas legal resources. Experienced researchers will find the book a useful reference for questions about the availability of particular types of authority in Texas and how to find them.

The book explores online legal research early, recognizing that students typically use online tools from the beginning of their studies. Since the researcher must understand print legal resources to research effectively either in print or online, the book first explains how to research each type of authority in print. Researching that type of authority online is then discussed. The book discusses the strengths and weaknesses of each format and suggests the more useful format for research in particular types of authority.

Texas Legal Research draws on the model developed by earlier books in the state legal research series. The series is based on the insight of series editor Suzanne E. Rowe, director of the legal writing program at the University of Oregon School of Law, that law students can best learn legal research from a concise study of research in the law of their state. I want to thank Suzanne Rowe, for the opportunity to write this book and for her invaluable advice and skillful editing. I must also thank Professor Rowe's research assistants, Ben Albers, Sara Buffie, Kelly Fahl, Laura Koths, Jun Lim, and Mason Whitcomb for their wonderful diligence and sharp eyes. My associate Mon Yin Lung provided thoughtful commentary on several of the more challenging issues. Thanks are also due to Professor James Hambleton, Associate Dean for Budget and Planning and Professor of Law at Texas Wesleyan University School of Law, for tips on the arcane subject of Texas writ and petition history. This book benefitted greatly from the counsel and support of these persons. Any errors or omissions are mine alone.

Spencer L. Simons
April 12, 2012

Texas Legal Research

Chapter 1

The Research Process and Legal Analysis

I. Texas Legal Research

The process of legal research is essentially the same in all states. The steps described and suggestions for managing the process contained in this chapter can be used successfully by any researcher in American law. The states do, however, differ in details of the substantive law, the law-making processes, the forms in which legal information is available, and the tools and techniques for finding the law. This text provides a thorough coverage of the sources of Texas law and of how to find and use each type of legal authority needed by the Texas legal researcher. The text also briefly explains federal legal research and variations in researching the law of other states.

II. Intersection of Legal Research and Legal Analysis

Although the researcher must be familiar with a large number of resources, the basic techniques of legal research are quite simple: use search terms to find documents in print or online resources and then locate additional documents cited in documents already found. The simplicity of the basic techniques does not make legal research a rote, mechanical process. All stages of the research process are guided by legal analysis and refined as the project progresses. The identification of legally relevant facts, legal theories, jurisdiction, and development

3

of search terms require legal analysis. Selection of the correct resources and searching them effectively turns on analysis, as does understanding the significance of documents found. The researcher will be constantly refining or changing her analysis throughout a project and pursuing research in the directions indicated as new insights are gained.

The research process should include repeated outlining of the analysis. The interdependence of research and analysis makes research challenging, especially for the person new to legal concepts and legal research resources. The aim of this book is to place Texas legal resources in the context of the structure of Texas government and law and teach a process best suited to give the novice researcher a firm analytical grounding early in a research project.

III. Types of Legal Authority

A. Primary and Secondary Authority

"Primary authority" is created by governmental bodies with law-making power. The structure of government and allocation of powers are determined by the constitution of the state or federal government. Legislatures create "statutes"; administrative agencies promulgate "rules" (sometime called "regulations"); and courts issue judicial "opinions" as they decide the issues before them. Statutes, administrative agency rules, and judicial opinions (commonly called "cases") are primary authority. The purpose of legal research is to find the controlling primary authority for an issue and predict how it will be applied to an issue.

"Secondary authority" summarizes, synthesizes, and comments on the law on some topic. Secondary authority, typically written by law professors, practitioners, and other legal experts, states what the law is on some topic, and sometimes proposes what the author thinks the law should be. Secondary authority includes treatises, practitioner guides, law review articles, and encyclopedias. It is often extremely useful for understanding complex or unfamiliar

Table 1-1. Examples of Authority in Texas Research

	Mandatory Authority	Persuasive Authority
Primary Authority	Texas Statutes Texas Supreme Court cases	Oklahoma statutes California Supreme Court cases
Secondary Authority	—	Law review articles Legal encyclopedias

areas of the law and finding primary law on a topic. Finding and studying secondary authority is often an essential stage of the research process.

B. Mandatory and Persuasive Authority

Some legal authority is binding on the courts as they decide disputes; it is "mandatory." Mandatory authority in Texas includes the state constitution, statutes and codes enacted by the legislature, rules promulgated by Texas administrative agencies, and published opinions of the Texas Supreme Court and Texas Court of Criminal Appeals.[1] The constitutions, statutes, rules, and judicial opinions of other states are not binding on Texas courts concerning matters of Texas law, but might be looked to by a court as "persuasive" authority. Thus, an Oklahoma statute or a decision from the Supreme Court of California would not be binding on a Texas court, but might be considered persuasive if relevant, well-reasoned, and concerning a matter not already controlled by Texas mandatory law. Secondary authority is never mandatory, but might be looked to by a court as persuasive authority. Table 1-1 illustrates the relationship of the mandatory and persuasive authority distinction to primary and secondary law.

---

1. An opinion of a Texas court of appeals is binding on Texas trial courts within its district if the particular topic has not been addressed by the Texas Supreme Court, for civil matters, or the Texas Court of Criminal Appeals, for criminal matters.

IV. Overview of the Research Process: The Seven-Step Process

Legal research projects are often complex and can easily go wrong if not approached systematically. The keys to effective research are structure and process. The researcher must understand the structure of government and the relationships between the legal texts produced by the various parts of government. These were introduced in the previous section of this chapter and are discussed at length in the rest of this book. The researcher must also have a plan for finding the texts and using them in the analysis of the issues researched. Effective research is a process that systematically locates primary authority in the most meaningful and efficient sequence and that encourages analysis. The seven-step process described below is the key to effective research for approaching a project in a complex or unfamiliar area of the law. Read it now for general understanding and return to it as you learn the research techniques for the types of legal authority to see how those techniques fit into the complete research process.

Step 1: Gather Facts and Develop Search Terms

The researcher will be presented with a situation that may call for a legal solution. Sometimes facts will already be summarized, as in a class assignment or a law firm assignment to an associate, or it may be necessary to draw out the facts, as a lawyer will do in interviewing a client. Facts mean little in themselves. Consider which of the facts known may be legally relevant. Consider also what further facts may be needed and try to ascertain them. Attempt to identify legal rules and theories that may apply to the facts presented. Consider also what jurisdiction's law is controlling. The researcher will thus develop lists of facts and legal concepts relating to the situation.

Use the facts and legal concepts to formulate a list of "search terms" to be used to search secondary and primary sources. Sup-

Table 1-2. Generating Research Terms

Journalistic Approach

Who:	Thief, robber, burglar, business owner, property owner
What:	Burglary, first degree, second degree, crime
How:	Breaking and entering, burglar tools, trespassing, darkness
Why:	Theft, stealing, stolen goods
When:	Midnight, night
Where:	Store, building, commercial establishment, business, shop

TARPP Approach

Things:	Burglar tool, stolen goods
Actions:	Burglary, breaking and entering, trespassing, damages, crime
Remedies:	First degree, second degree, incarceration
People:	Thief, robber, burglar, business owner, property owner
Places:	Store, building, commercial establishment, business, shop

plement the list of search terms by brainstorming with questions designed to elicit additional search terms. Some people prefer to use the journalist's who, what, how, why, when, and where questions, while others use the TARPP approach: things, actions, remedies, people, and places. Whether one of these approaches or another is used, the researcher will develop a list of terms to describe potentially relevant facts, legal issues, and possible solutions.

As an example, assume you are working for a defense attorney who was recently assigned to a burglary case. Your client allegedly bent a credit card to spring the lock to a stereo store and stole $2,000 worth of equipment. The store's security system showed an intrusion at about midnight. Your client is charged with first-degree burglary. The question you have been asked to research is whether there is a good argument for limiting the charge to second-degree burglary if a burglary is committed with a credit card and not with professional burglar tools. Table 1-2 provides examples of research terms you might use to begin your research.

As the research project progresses, you will discover new "terms of art" (unique legal terms) as well as words or phrases commonly used to describe concepts in the particular topic area. If searches yield too few results, consider broader terms. If searches yield too many results, consider narrower terms. The need to ascertain other legally significant facts may also appear as applicable legal rules are more fully understood. Add any new words, phrases, and factual terms to the list of search terms.

Step 2: Search in Secondary Sources

The search terms developed in Step 1 are used to search in secondary sources, such as encyclopedias, treatises, practice guides, or law reviews. In print resources, these terms will be used to search "indexes" for references to discussion of your topic. An index is an alphabetical list of terms identifying the topics addressed in a work or collection of works, with page numbers or other identifiers indicating where the topic is located. In online resources, the terms may be used to formulate queries to search the text of databases or to search online versions of the indexes to the resources.

Step 3: Research Constitutional, Statutory, and Administrative Law

After reading secondary authority, the researcher will usually have a good idea whether constitutional, statutory, or administrative law affects the analysis. Specific cites to primary authority found in Step 2 must be located and read. Since the authority cited in the secondary sources might not be comprehensive, the researcher will also conduct a complete search using the updated list of search terms. Begin in an annotated code, using the techniques explained in Chapters 3 and 6, to find references to relevant constitutional and statutory law, and the techniques in Chapter 8 to find administrative agency rules. Be sure to update all law found immediately.

Step 4: Find Judicial Opinions

Once controlling constitutional provisions, statutes, or administrative agency rules have been found, it is necessary to find judicial opinions interpreting the meaning and verifying the legitimacy of those authorities. The annotated codes and constitutions used in Step 3 provide many cites. Additional cases may be located using "digests." Digests are collections of case abstracts classified by topic, allowing essentially all cases on a particular topic within a jurisdiction to be found. In those instances where the law is entirely judge-made common law, cases may be found using online searches in case databases, as in Westlaw or LexisNexis, or by using digests. If cases are found in online databases using full-text searches, it is essential to perform additional searches using digests or the tools described in Chapter 5 to identify cases the database searches missed. All cases found and considered relevant must be updated immediately using an online citator, such as Westlaw's KeyCite or LexisNexis' Shepard's citators. Citators may also reveal additional relevant cases.

Step 5: Read Judicial Opinions Carefully

Before reading a case, skim the text to determine which parts of the case are relevant to your research project. Many cases discuss a number of topics. Read the relevant cases carefully and take notes summarizing each useful case. Synthesize from the relevant cases a statement of the rule developed by courts of the jurisdiction in the opinions. Consider alternative interpretations of the case law that may support your client's position or that of your opponent. A critical part of advocacy is anticipating how your opponent will argue the law should be construed.

Step 6: Update All Authority

Update all primary authority relied upon in your analysis. Use online citators to update case law and much statutory law. Updating of certain types of authority may require other techniques, described in the chapter in this book discussing that kind of authority.

Step 7: When to Stop Researching

Stop researching when no additional relevant authorities are being found and your analysis is complete. If no authority has been found on some issues, review your research journal (discussed in Part V.B.) to make sure no steps or resources have been overlooked.

V. Control of the Research Process

A. Research Strategy

Since many legal topics are complex, it is usually necessary to begin research in secondary sources, such as encyclopedias, treatises, or practitioner guides. The process can be varied, however. The researcher might already be familiar with the area of law, or perhaps the person assigning the project has stated that the controlling law is statutory. The researcher might in such instances start by researching in the statutes. If an issue is clearly one of common law, the researcher might even begin by searching in case law. The person new to the law and legal research seldom has the legal background to confidently bypass steps in the seven-step process. It is important to understand that proceeding immediately to searching for cases, as in Westlaw or LexisNexis case databases, is very likely to lead to serious errors.

Although the research process presented here has seven distinct steps, the process is not linear. As more is learned, it is often necessary to revisit earlier steps. Cases might refer to statutes or regulations not previously found. New insights gained from reading mandatory authority might send you back to the secondary authorities for further and deeper reading. Updating of cases might reveal new cases or law review articles that should be read. Outlining and writing often reveal unanswered questions that must be researched to complete the analysis. It is critical that no steps in the process be missed, but it is almost certain that steps will be revisited as more is learned.

B. The Research Journal

A research project requires finding and organizing a lot of material and recording evaluations and use of the materials found. Stacks of copies, printouts, and loose notes can rapidly get out of control. At the core of the research process will be a "journal," a log of all actions taken during the project. It is also a good idea to use files to accumulate certain types of materials, such as copies of statutes, lists of primary authority citations, or notes on cases read. The organizational methods will vary by project and personal preferences. Some researchers prefer to keep all or most of their records in paper and to handwrite their notes. Other researchers do everything electronically. The important thing is to have a system that organizes materials and allows effective review, retrieval, and planning. Following are a few tips that apply to almost all projects:

Start the journal with lists of facts, search terms, and issues presented. All of these can be supplemented and revised as more is learned.

Formulate the initial strategy, including which steps of the seven-step process to pursue in this project, the time period to be researched, and the time and budget available for the project.

Record all actions taken, including every resource checked, the search terms used, and the results of each search.

Take notes. It is tempting to just copy or print materials found for later reading. In the end, extensive copying and printing wastes not just paper and printing costs, but time and quality. Assimilation and analysis occurs throughout the research process. Skim materials as you locate them, read the relevant parts, and take notes on what you have read. Taking notes forces you to select, to think, and to summarize. In the process, your analysis is developing and will lead you to ask the questions and consider the possibilities that lead to new discoveries and direct your efforts most effectively.

Record full citations for all materials to be located. Few things are more frustrating than not being able to find something needed or having to spend time tracking down complete citation information at the last minute.

Especially when reading statutes or regulations, follow up on all cross-references in the text immediately. If you do not read definitions or other statutes or regulations referred to in the text, you cannot understand the statute or regulation before you.

Write down all insights and questions to pursue as they occur to you, perhaps in a special page of your journal.

C. Read, Analyze, and Outline

Read and analyze the relevant portions of primary authority as you find them. Update the authority immediately to make sure you are working with current law. When you read a statute, outline it in your notes to make sure you understand it. If you cannot outline it, you don't understand it. Similarly, summarize cases you read and keep the summary and full citation where they can easily be retrieved.

Outline your analysis early and often. Your first outline will be incomplete and tentative, but the process of outlining achieves several goals. Outlining forces you to formulate your analysis. The analysis will state the issue, give the rule determined in your research, apply the facts to the rule, and draw a conclusion. In addition, outlining tests your understanding and reveals gaps in the facts or your knowledge of the law. If you cannot outline the analysis so that no gaps remain, you need to understand more about the law or identify the missing facts necessary to the analysis. Finally, outlining prepares you to write. Once you have a complete outline with no gaps, organized in a logical manner, you are ready to write. Starting to write without an outline is very likely to lead to trouble, as you discover too late (or your reader does) that your analysis is not complete or presented most effectively.

Once you have written your first draft, review it and rewrite. If time allows, let the draft sit for a day or two before reviewing and rewriting. Errors and omissions that were not evident while you were writing are often obvious when the draft has had a chance to rest. Finally, as soon as possible before submitting your work product, update all authority relied upon once again.

VI. Organization of This Book

The remainder of this book explains how to conduct research in a variety of sources. A subject of major concern for many researchers, including students and teachers, is when to use online research tools and how to use them most effectively. Since the question arises very early in research instruction, and the techniques of online instruction are referred to throughout the book, Chapter 2 explains online searching techniques and issues.

Although research generally begins with secondary sources, this book next addresses research in primary law, since finding primary law is the ultimate goal of legal research. Each chapter focuses on Texas legal authority and sources, with research in federal law and the law of other states discussed briefly. Chapter 3 addresses research in constitutions, the highest law of any jurisdiction. Chapters 4 and 5 deal with the court system and searching for judicial opinions. Chapters 6 and 7 deal with statutory research and searching for documents produced in the legislative process. Chapter 8 addresses research in the law produced by administrative agencies.

Following the discussion of research in types of primary law, other important resources are examined. Chapter 9 explains the use of citators to determine whether primary law is still "good law" and to locate additional documents. Chapter 10 discusses the use of major secondary resources. Finally, Appendix A provides a basic guide to citation of legal materials and Appendix B provides a bibliography of other books on the subjects of legal research and analysis. The general research texts focus on research in federal legal materials and thus complement the focus of this book on Texas legal research.

Chapter 2

Online Legal Research

I. Introduction

The structure of legal information and the research process were developed before computers. Many research projects can still be conducted almost entirely in print in a well-stocked law library. Almost all primary U.S. legal authority is now available online, as is a great deal of secondary authority. The researcher must decide whether to research in print or online and, if searching online, which online providers to use. Experienced researchers choose the format and source best suited to the research task before them. This chapter focuses first on factors to consider in making the choice between print and online research. The remainder of the chapter discusses techniques for effective and cost-effective online searching.

II. Choosing Between Online or Print Resources

A. Where Is the Document Available?

Do not assume that all necessary resources are available online. Virtually all recent primary authority and some older primary authority documents are available online. Many older documents needed by the researcher are, however, available only in print. Essential secondary sources might be available only in print, although they are increasingly available online. Certain finding tools and updating tools are available only online.

B. Is an Online Document Official and Verifiable?

Any document of primary authority relied upon or cited must be official, meaning the document is identified by the government as having been issued by a government body or agent with the authority to create law. The document must also be verifiable, meaning the text is, in fact, that declared to be official by the government and the text has not been altered. The fixed nature of print publication made determining whether a document was official and verifying the accuracy of the text relatively easy. Verifying the official status and unaltered nature of online publications is more difficult. Many documents placed on government websites are explicitly stated to not be official, with the user often being referred to an official print publication for verification. Any document reproduced on non-government websites must also be viewed with caution, since electronic documents are easily altered. A major advantage of using recognized legal information vendors, such as LexisNexis or Westlaw, is that they undertake to procure and deliver the official documents and they stake their reputations upon doing this reliably.

C. What Is the Database Scope?

Before searching in an online database, determine its "scope," which means what the database includes. For example, a database of law journal articles might contain only articles since 1980. The researcher not aware of this limitation might miss important articles. The "scope note" for a database commonly lists the publications included, the types of articles included, and the dates covered. Tips for searching the database may also be included. Look for a link to the scope note before using any unfamiliar database. In Westlaw and LexisNexis, a button with an "i" is the link to the scope note.

D. How Current Is the Source?

Although online databases are potentially the most current of all resources, it is essential to determine how recently a database has been updated. Many websites have a note at the bottom of the page stating when the page was last updated. Scope notes often give a date of last update or the cut-off dates for documents in a database. A related question is how soon information is included in a database. For example, some periodicals can only be published online after an embargo period, meaning they cannot be published online for some period after the appearance of the print publication. Where publication is embargoed, the researcher may need to locate an article in print.

E. What Is the Cost/Time Tradeoff?

Many choices between formats turn on economic decisions. Some online resources are very efficient, but very expensive. Other databases may require more time to search, but be less expensive. The choice to use one or the other database may turn on how urgent the request is and the budget available for a project. The materials in an online database are probably also available in print. If the print version is close at hand, it may be more economical to use that version than to conduct expensive online searches and printing. If access to the print version would require travel, the online choice might be more economical. The researcher with access to an academic or law firm library should also consider that the print has been paid for, so there is no extra cost for each use, while the online searches might require considerable outlays for each search and download.

F. How Easy Is Searching and Navigating?

Some resources are easier to search online, while others are more readily searched in print. For example, many experienced researchers find online searching in statutes and regulations more difficult and less effective than searching in print.

Once relevant documents are identified, some are easier to use online and some are easier in print. Online documents might have links to related parts or to other documents, making navigation quick and easy. On the other hand, some resources are easier to move back and forth in and to see the relationships between the various parts in print. Statutes are an example of a resource many researchers find easier to navigate in print.

G. How Easy Is Reading and Scanning?

You may find print is easier to read and scan for certain purposes. Prolonged, extensive reading is often done more easily in print. For example, many people prefer to do preliminary reading in secondary resources in print, even if an online search was used to locate the resource. Good researchers are generally experts at skimming large amounts of text in order to identify relevant portions of extensive works. Many people find that rapid skimming can be done much more effectively in print.

A related issue is that reading resources in print makes it much easier to keep track of the kind of resources you are using. Documents of different types can appear very similar on a computer screen. The potential for confusion is increased by the ease with which clicking on links can bring the reader to very different types of documents, making it easy to lose the context and the relationship between the documents. Familiarity with the types of legal documents gained from using them in print ultimately allows better control of research in the online environment.

H. Do You Need to Print, Email, or Cut and Paste?

A great advantage of researching in online resources is the ease with which text can be extracted, copied, and transmitted. When it is necessary to capture large blocks of text for later use, to quickly transmit to another person or location, or to quickly cut and paste into new documents, online resources are much more useful than print versions of the same resources. The ease of using these capacities may, however, cause problems when the need is to read closely, develop deep understanding, and synthesize what is being read. As noted above, close reading is often done better in print than online.

III. Online Resources

A. Westlaw and LexisNexis

Westlaw and LexisNexis are the predominant online vendors of legal information. Each has vast collections of primary and secondary legal material, as well as extensive news sources, public records information, and practice tools. LexisNexis, now owned by Elsevier, is descended from Lexis, the first venture into computer-assisted legal research. Westlaw was developed by the dominant legal publisher, West, in response to the introduction of Lexis. West is now owned by another publishing giant, Thomson Reuters. LexisNexis and Westlaw continue to expand their contents and to develop their search capacities. As a result, LexisNexis and Westlaw are extremely expensive sources of legal information.

B. Free Online Legal Resources

Many lawyers and law firms cannot afford to use Westlaw or LexisNexis, or use them only when other resources are not sufficient. Many researchers reduce their legal research costs by using the increasing numbers of free online legal materials provided at the websites of governmental bodies, educational institutions, and other organizations. Many resources can be found through the major online directories to free online legal information. Prominent directories are the Library of Congress' Guide to Law Online, at www.loc.gov/law/help, and Cornell University's Legal Information Institute (L.I.I.), at www.law.cornell.edu.

C. Other Commercial Databases

Several commercial online legal research sites compete with LexisNexis and Westlaw. The information supplied by these vendors is less extensive and their searching capacities tend to be less refined than those of Westlaw and LexisNexis. They are, however, considerably less expensive than Westlaw and LexisNexis. Westlaw and LexisNexis have responded to this competition by offering inex-

Table 2-1. Commercial Legal Database Provider

Provider	Web Address
Casemaker	www.TexasBarCLE.com
(free to State Bar of Texas members)	
LexisNexis	www.lexisnexis.com
Loislaw	www.loislaw.com
TheLaw.net	http://thelaw.net
VersusLaw	www.versuslaw.com
Westlaw	www.westlaw.com

pensive subscriptions with limited content. These subscriptions typically provide access to primary law of one state, federal primary law, essential secondary materials for a state, and access to the online citator.[1] The sole practitioner or small law firm should consider these less expensive alternatives. See Table 2-1 for a list of online commercial database providers. Keep an eye out for new legal information providers, as services with innovative search tools attempt to enter the market.

D. Specialized Legal Databases

Westlaw and LexisNexis provide access to vast amounts of legal information, but they do not provide everything the legal researcher needs. Other commercial vendors provide subscriptions to specialized legal information. Examples are Bloomberg BNA (B.N.A.), C.C.H. (a division of Wolters Kluwer), and Thomson Reuters/RIA (R.I.A.), which provide online databases on such specialized topics as health law, business and finance, and tax law. Each of these has long been a prominent publisher of legal infor-

---

1. Chapter 9 discusses Westlaw's KeyCite and LexisNexis' Shepard's citation services.

mation. Many of their online resources are adapted from their existing publications. Academic and law firm libraries subscribe to specialized legal databases. Be sure to examine your library's web pages to determine which online legal resources are available.

IV. Keyword Searching in Westlaw and LexisNexis

Computerized databases revolutionized legal research by making it possible to search for specific words in vast collections of documents. Full-text, searchable databases are developed by programs that identify each word in documents in the database and record in a master index the occurrence of each word and its unique location. When a word is entered in a search query, the computer searches the master index and all documents containing that word are reported in the search results. By combining words and using operators defining the logical relationship or proximity of the words to each other in a document, very sophisticated searches can be performed.

In the early days of computerized research, many researchers believed this "keyword" searching would eliminate the need for the traditional finding tools developed for searching in print. This proved not to be the case. Problems with keyword searching are discussed in Section C. of this part. Responses to the weaknesses of keyword searching are discussed in Part V.

A. Terms and Connectors Searching

Westlaw, LexisNexis, and other computerized legal research services provide the capacity to search using "terms and connectors." Such queries consist of search terms and connectors expressing logical relationships between the search terms, the proximity of the terms to each other, or other features of the terms. The system of expressing logical relationships between terms is known as "Boolean" logic searching. The symbols used for the

Table 2-2. Westlaw and LexisNexis Connectors and Commands

Goal	LexisNexis	Westlaw
To find alternative terms anywhere in the document	or	or blank space
To find both terms anywhere in the document	and &	and &
To find both terms within a particular distance from each other	/p = in 1 paragraph /s = in 1 sentence /n = within a certain number of words	/p = in 1 paragraph /s = in 1 sentence /n = within a certain number of words
To find terms used as a phrase	leave a blank space between each word	put the phrase in quotation marks
To control the hierarchy of searching	parentheses	parentheses
To exclude terms	and not	but not %
To extend the end of a term	!	!
To hold the place of letters in a term	*	*

connectors differ somewhat between the services. Table 2-2 compares the symbols used by Westlaw and LexisNexis for common connectors and commands. Many of the commands work the same in either Westlaw or LexisNexis, but some, such as leaving spaces between words without putting quotation marks around them, work very differently in the two services.[2] Other online services use different connectors and commands for Boolean logic

---

2. In Westlaw, the terms *judicial* and *notice* with a space between them would be read by the search engine as logically identical to: *judicial* or *notice*. In LexisNexis, the same query would be read by the search engine as identical to the phrase: "*judicial notice*."

Figure 2-1. Natural Language Search in Westlaw

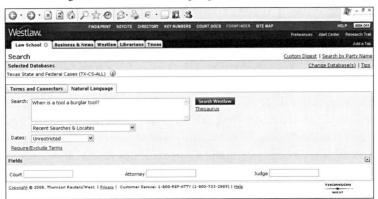

Source: Westlaw. Reprinted with permission of Thomson Reuters.

searching. The researcher must use the "Help" feature of an unfamiliar online database service to learn the connectors and commands for forming queries in that service before beginning to search.

B. Natural Language Searching

LexisNexis and Westlaw provide "natural language" searching as an alternative to terms and connectors keyword searching. Natural language searching allows the searcher to enter a question, short sentence, or string of search terms as a query. The program converts this unstructured query into a form the search engine can use and returns results ranked by relevance. Although some users consider this method easier than forming terms and connectors queries, the searcher does not know just what the program is doing or why results are identified as relevant. Experienced researchers often prefer to use natural language searching as a backup when terms and connectors searches are not yielding good results or to identify additional documents not captured by terms and connectors searches. Figure 2-1 shows a natural language query in Westlaw. Note that terms and connectors searches can be entered by clicking on the "Terms and Connectors" tab.

C. Problems with Keyword Searching

The hope that keyword searching could completely replace such traditional tools as indexes and tables of contents was not realized. Studies of computer searching effectiveness have revealed that even skilled researchers often find only a small percentage of the relevant documents in a database. There are several reasons for the problems with keyword searching. First, the researcher often cannot think of all terms that might be used to identify relevant concepts. Next, a search that captures a large percentage of relevant documents also tends to capture very large numbers of irrelevant documents, making identification of the relevant documents in a large "hit list" impractical. One of the most challenging problems is that text expressing a concept might not contain any words directly representing that concept. Consider how traditional stories, such as folk tales or parables, express abstract concepts. A particular problem for the legal researcher is that useful analogies might be found in cases with very different facts and using different terms than those the researcher has thought of.

V. Getting the Most from Keyword Searching

A. Using Segments and Fields

Searching for the appearance of keywords in the complete texts in a database may yield many irrelevant hits, while a search limited to just certain parts of each document may be much more focused. For example, if each article in a database contains abstracts of the full article, the abstracts will probably contain the most relevant terms. If the database allows searching just in the abstracts, relevant articles can be found, while avoiding many articles with those terms appearing in irrelevant contexts in the body of the article. Searches in the title segment may allow similar focus. Westlaw uses the term "fields." LexisNexis uses "segments."

The database developers might also have developed fields containing just one kind of information from the documents, such as au-

Figure 2-2. Fields in Westlaw

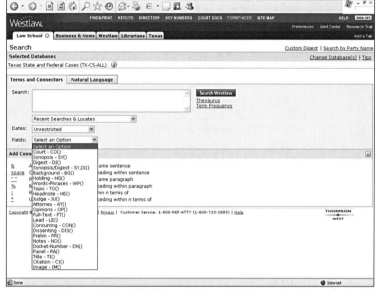

Source: Westlaw. Reprinted with permission of Thomson Reuters.

thor, publisher, or subject. For court opinions, fields for judges, attorneys, or docket numbers allow focused searching. Another feature often provided is the limiting of searches by date range or by type of publication. Figure 2-2 shows the fields that can be selected for focused searching in the Texas cases database on Westlaw. The particular fields available vary by database. Note also the list of connectors, partially obscured by the list of fields, and the bar for entering date restrictions.

B. Refining Queries

Carefully consider search strategy before beginning to enter queries. The initial query should include the terms believed most likely to be found in the document, with connectors representing the most likely relationships of the terms. Must both terms appear in a relevant document? If so, will they probably appear in the same sentence? In that case, a search structured A /s B might be a good place to start. This search may be too narrow and produce too few or no results. Plan what to do if the search needs to be broadened. Synonyms for terms A and B should be identified and added as alternatives, producing a query such as (A or C) /s (B or D or E). The search could also be broadened by changing the proximity operator, so the terms need only be in the same paragraph or even in the entire document.

A strategy for broadening and narrowing queries should be developed before beginning the search, since searching in Westlaw and LexisNexis is very expensive and must be performed with maximum efficiency. Law students should use their subsidized access during their years in school to practice the methods that will allow them to be efficient, low-cost searchers in practice.

VI. Add Power to the Search with Finding Tools

Full-text searching with keywords works very well for some searches and very poorly at other times. Since legal researchers must be able to locate all relevant documents, not just some, legal database providers have increasingly recognized the need to supply other finding tools. These finding tools were developed to locate information in print resources but have proven equally useful for online searching.

A. Indexes

Indexes have long been used to point the researcher to information in books and in bodies of literature, such as law journal articles. Good indexes are created by indexing specialists, with subject expertise and knowledge of how people look for information. The indexer considers the concepts and terms researchers will use to find material on a subject. An index created with the insight of a human indexer will often point the researcher to information that would not be found by a simple keyword search of a computer database's master index.

When searching for legal documents, check whether an index is available. The index may be supplied by the vendor as an alternative search mode for a database, such as a code database on Westlaw. Such an index can typically be either skimmed online or searched for words within the index. There are also online indexes developed to search entire bodies of literature. For example, LegalTrac, based on the print *Current Law Index*, is a popular database for searching for legal periodical literature.

B. Tables of Contents

Tables of contents are another type of finding tool. Reviewing the table of contents to a work may reveal material not found either by searching in the index or by conducting a keyword search. Tables of contents are now commonly included as an option for searching many online databases. For example, the statutory codes in Westlaw and LexisNexis often include a table of contents identical to that in the print versions.

C. West's Key Number System and LexisNexis' Topic and Headnote System

The West Key Number System and the Topic and Headnote System developed by LexisNexis are powerful tools for extending a search from cases found by a keyword search, or from other sources, to find many more cases on the same subject. Effective use of these tools compensates for the often incomplete coverage from searching only with keyword searches. These powerful tools are discussed at much greater length in Chapter 5, Researching Judicial Opinions.

D. Citators: KeyCite and Shepard's

Westlaw's KeyCite and LexisNexis' Shepard's are "citators." They are most often used to identify cases that have cited a particular case, but they also identify references citing statutes, regulations, patents, administrative decisions, and law journals in a number of primary and secondary resources (be sure to check exactly which resources are included within the citator being used). Thus, the researcher who has found a case or other document can extend the results of the search by using KeyCite or Shepard's to identify other relevant documents. Citators are very useful in the later stages of research to identify cases or other documents that have been missed by other search techniques. KeyCite and Shepard's are discussed at length in Chapter 9, Updating with Citators.

VII. Cost-Effective Searching

As noted previously, Westlaw and LexisNexis are very expensive research tools. Although law students have unlimited access to Westlaw and LexisNexis while in school, they will be expected to be cost-effective researchers in practice. A number of techniques can lower the cost of online searching.

Use free online material. Much primary authority available on Westlaw or LexisNexis is also available at government and non-profit websites. If only the text of a judicial opinion is needed, for example, that opinion might be found at the website of the issuing court.

Read offline when possible. Reading online can be expensive. If you have access to a law library, remember that the casebooks, statutes, treatises, and other materials in the library have already been paid for, so using those resources incurs no further costs. Rather than read documents online, consider downloading or printing the list of cites found by the search and going offline to read the documents in the library, at free websites, or printed from the database.

Use the best contract for the purpose. Westlaw and LexisNexis make their services available under various contractual terms. Some contracts are more economical for prolonged online reading, while others allow numerous searches at lower cost. A law firm or legal department may have more than one contract. The researcher in a law firm or legal department should know the terms of the contracts and search using the contracts most economical for the particular purpose.

Search in the narrowest database containing what you seek. Narrow databases generally cost less to search than do more inclusive databases. If cases from only a single state or federal court are sought, searching in Westlaw's ALLCASES database will cost more per search, as well as return many irrelevant results. Be sure a database contains what you are looking for before incurring the cost of a search. Check the scope note before using any unfamiliar database.

Formulate your queries carefully before logging on. A single search on Westlaw or LexisNexis may cost well over a hundred dollars. Plan how you will broaden or narrow your query if your initial results are too broad or too narrow. Before hitting the enter button, review the query you have written to make sure everything is spelled right, connectors are properly used, and all parentheses are closed.

Use the "Locate in results" feature in Westlaw or FOCUS in Lexis-Nexis. Once a query has been entered and a hit list returned, the documents in that list can be searched for the presence of additional terms at no extra cost. Using Locate in results or FOCUS to find a term in a set of documents is much more cost-effective than conducting a revised search.

Save your searches. Queries and search results can be saved using "Research Trail" on Westlaw or "History" in LexisNexis. Keeping track of searches run helps prevent time-wasting replication of work already done. As discussed in Chapter 1, all searches should be recorded in a research journal.

Minimize printing. Print only what you will need. Consider using the books in the library rather than making costly printouts. For large amounts of material, save results to a flash drive or email them to yourself for later review. Be sure you know what will print before hitting "print." Are you printing the cite list or the full text of all documents? If working in an annotated code, are you printing just the text of the statute or all the annotations? The difference can be hundreds of pages.

VIII. Pitfalls of Online Searching and Solutions

Online legal research has brought great speed and flexibility to the research process. Properly used, online research allows doing more, faster. The very nature of online research can, however, lead the inexperienced researcher into serious mistakes.

A. Tunnel Vision and "Law-Bytes"[3]

Experts in legal research instruction have noted that researchers using online resources are prone to focus on isolated portions of text in a document, without awareness of its relationship to the overall text. It is not uncommon, for example, for novice researchers to cite a case as supporting a certain point based on the court's discussion of the reasoning of other courts' decisions or of hypotheticals. Such citations are generally wrong and may even be totally opposite to the actual holding of the case. A related problem is a tendency of researchers to focus on an isolated block of text as the meaning of the case, rather than perceive the subtleties of the full analysis. These problems stem, at least in part, from reading documents on a computer screen, making it more difficult to keep the larger context in mind.

A solution to this problem is to do a thorough and close reading of the document in print, whether printed out from the database or in books. The temptation to cut and paste blocks of text as a substitute for careful consideration and analysis can be combatted by developing habits of note-taking and analytical summarization throughout the research process.

---

3. The term "law-byte" was introduced in Molly Warner Lien, *Essay, Technocentrism and the Soul of the Common Law Lawyer*, 48 Am. U. L. Rev. 85, 88 (1998).

B. Inadvertent Plagiarism

Plagiarism, the unattributed use of the words or concepts of another, is a problem in all kinds of research. Even unintended plagiarism can destroy a career. It is particularly easy to fall into the trap of unintentional plagiarism when portions of text are being cut and pasted from many resources.

The solution is to observe in computer research the same standards of recording the origin of quoted text that are observed in working with print resources. Be sure to include with all copied text a full citation to the origin of the text. Placing all cut and pasted text, together with full cites, in the research journal will help prevent later misuse of the text. Placing the cut and pasted text into the research journal also encourages its use in the analytical process. Resist the temptation to cut and paste text from a document directly to a draft of a research paper. If you lose track of what has been borrowed this way and fail to attribute the source, the penalties may be severe.

C. Losing Track

The power of online research is enhanced by the ability to link from cites in a document to the cited documents. Linking allows the instantaneous review of related documents, but it also allows the researcher to leap from document to document, possibly losing track of the path followed and relationship between the documents. This can result in confusion and much wasted time and expense.

The researcher in Westlaw or LexisNexis can view the Research Trail or History as a reminder. Even more effective is keeping track of every step in the research trail in the research journal, with notes on the significance of what is found at each step.

Chapter 3

Constitutional Law

I. Introduction

A constitution is the foundational primary law document of a state or nation. All other laws must conform to the requirements of the constitution. While the United States of America has had but one constitution, amended infrequently, the State of Texas has had several, with the current constitution containing numerous and frequent amendments.

The constitutional history of Texas reflects a dramatic state history. Since all aspects of Texas law and Texas legal authorities have been affected by key events in Texas history, the researcher in Texas law must be familiar with certain events. This chapter begins with that history and then moves to the process of researching constitutional law.

II. A Thumbnail History of Texas and Its Constitution

A familiar statement about Texas is that six flags have flown over it: the flags of France, Spain, Mexico, the Republic of Texas, the Confederacy, and the United States. France claimed the territory that is now Texas from 1685 to 1762, while Spanish exploration, claims, and colonization occurred fitfully, particularly after 1700. The boundaries between French claims and Spanish claims in the New World were indistinct.

After the purchase of French territory by the United States, the boundary between Spanish Mexico and the United States was established as the Red and Sabine Rivers by the Treaty of 1819. In 1821, Mexico declared independence from Spain, and the first grants of Mexican territory to Anglo-American colonizers were made in 1822. In 1824, Mexico established a constitutional, federal form of government, under which the regions of Coahuila and Texas were joined into a single state. The new state contained tensions from the start: the constitution of the state of Coahuila and Texas forbade slavery, made Catholicism the state religion, and did not grant a right to trial by jury. Further, all laws were published only in Spanish. The largely Anglo-American population of Texas resented these and other provisions by the numerically dominant Mexican population of Coahuila. In 1834, General Antonio López de Santa Anna overthrew the Mexican constitutional government and established himself as dictator.

The increasingly restive population of Texas declared independence from Mexico on March 2, 1836;[1] fought and defeated the forces led against Texas by Santa Anna; and established the independent Republic of Texas, with a constitution ratified in September of 1836. In 1840, the common law of England was formally received and all laws in effect prior to September 1, 1836, were repealed, except for certain laws implemented during the period of the Provisional Government and laws relating to grants, land colonization, and mines and minerals.[2]

The Constitution of 1836 contained an extensive Bill of Rights; many of its provisions have been carried forward through successive constitutions to the present constitution in their original wordings. Texas was admitted to the Union in 1845 and a new Constitution of 1845 was ratified.

Texas seceded from the Union in 1861, with a revised Constitution of 1861 largely based on the 1845 constitution. After the end of the

---

1. Coahuila also seceded from Mexico, joining with Nuevo Leon and Tamaulipas to form the Republic of the Rio Grande.

2. Researchers into land and mineral rights must still sometimes refer to pre-Republic Spanish and Mexican law and documents to determine present-day rights.

Table 3-1. Articles of the Constitution of the State of Texas 1876

	Preamble.
Article I.	Bill of Rights.
Article II.	The Powers of Government.
Article III.	Legislative Department.
Article IV.	Executive Department.
Article V.	Judicial Department.
Article VI.	Suffrage.
Article VII.	Education.
Article VIII.	Taxation and Revenue.
Article IX.	Counties.
Article X.	Railroads.
Article XI.	Municipal Corporations.
Article XII.	Private Corporations.
Article XIII.	Spanish and Mexican Land Titles. (repealed)
Article XIV.	Public Lands and Land Office.
Article XV.	Impeachment.
Article XVI.	General Provisions.
Article XVII.	Mode of Amending the Constitution of This State.

Civil War, the federal government imposed a military government on Texas under the Reconstruction Act of 1867, invalidating the Constitution of 1866; that constitution had reflected in its provisions the secessionist sympathies of its drafters. The subsequent Constitution of 1869 was a product of the Reconstruction period and much disliked by the majority of Texans at the time.

The present constitution, the Constitution of 1876, took effect on April 18, 1876. The Constitution of 1876 in its present form is very long, over 200 pages, containing much detail that would normally be considered statutory in nature. See Table 3-1 for a list of the seventeen articles of the Constitution of 1876. This length and detail reflected a tendency in state constitutions in the nineteenth century, as well as a reaction against abuses by officials and judges during the Reconstruction period: many constitutional provisions were intended to limit the discretion of officials. The length and detail of the Constitution of 1876 also result from the fact that it has been frequently amended, from its inception up to the present time. As of 2012, the constitution had been amended 474 times.[3] The amendments have changed the language in the body of the constitution itself, rather than being appended at the end, as are the amendments to the Constitution of the United States.

III. Finding the Texas Constitution

The Texas constitution can be found in several places. Online sources for the constitution are discussed in Part VI. of this chapter. The most useful source of the Constitution of the State of Texas for legal research is *Vernon's Annotated Constitution of the State of Texas (Annotated Constitution)*.[4]

A. Contents of *Vernon's Annotated Constitution of the State of Texas*

Most of the eight-volume set of *Vernon's Annotated Constitution of the State of Texas* consists of the current text of the constitution, with annotations containing much useful information about the history and interpretation of the constitution. The final volume in *Vernon's Annotated Constitution of the State of Texas* includes historical essays and documents relating to the formation of the Republic of Texas and its independence, accession to statehood, and secession from the Union. The full texts of the Constitutions of 1836, 1845, 1861, 1866, and 1869 are included. For background and comparison, the volume also includes the Magna Carta, United States Declaration of Independence, the Articles of Confederation, and the Constitution of the United States. For quick reference and easy reading, the Constitution

---

3. *Constitutional Amendments*, Legislative Reference Library of Texas, www.lrl.state.tx.us/legis/constAmends/index.cfm.

4. The eight volumes are part of the *Vernon's* set, a West publication, which also contains the annotated statutes and court rules discussed in Chapter 6. *Vernon's* is readily recognizable in any Texas collection as the large set of black books.

of the United States is printed in its entirety at the front of the first volume of the *Annotated Constitution*.

B. Finding Relevant Constitutional Provisions in *Vernon's*

To find relevant provisions of the Constitution of the State of Texas, begin with an index. There is an index provided specifically for the constitution in volume 8; the general index at the end of the *Vernon's* set contains references to the constitution as well as statutes and other enacted law. Another approach is to use the table of contents in volume 1 of the *Annotated Constitution* set.

The Constitution of the State of Texas is numbered with articles and sections. To find a particular provision, pull the volume containing the relevant article, and then find the specific section. Read this language very carefully, as it is the highest law in the state. Figure 3-1 shows an article and section of the Texas Constitution in *Vernon's*.

C. Using the Annotations in *Vernon's*

Each provision of the constitution is followed by annotations. Annotations, discussed at length in Chapter 6 on statutory research, are added research references that aid in the understanding of each section of the constitution. After each section, the editors have added such enhancements as historical notes, interpretive commentary, cross-references to other parts of the constitution or Texas statutes, the location of equivalent sections in the earlier constitutions, citations to law review and journal articles and other secondary commentary and practice aids, and, very importantly, the "Notes of Decisions." Figure 3-2 shows annotations to the constitutional section in Figure 3-1. Note particularly the case summaries under Notes of Decisions at the bottom of Figure 3-2.

The annotations help the researcher locate resources to analyze the constitution. The Historical Notes and Interpretive Commentary cast

Figure 3-1. Article and Section of the Texas
Constitution in *Vernon's*

ARTICLE XII

PRIVATE CORPORATIONS

Section
1. Creation by general laws.
2. General laws to be enacted; protection of public and stockholders.
3 to 5. Repealed.
6. Repealed.
7. Repealed.

Westlaw Computer Assisted Legal Research

Westlaw supplements your legal research in many ways. Westlaw allows you to

- update your research with the most current information
- expand your library with additional resources
- retrieve current, comprehensive history and citing references to a case with KeyCite

For more information on using Westlaw to supplement your research, see the Westlaw Electronic Research Guide, which follows the Preface.

---

§ 1. Creation by general laws

Sec. 1.   No private corporation shall be created except by general laws.

INTERPRETIVE COMMENTARY

In post-Revolutionary War America, there was universal agreement that the power to form corporations, which in England belonged to both king and parliament, was lodged solely in the legislatures. Statutory authority was therefore requisite to the creation of any corporation. This concept was part of the stock of ideas carried into Texas by its Anglo-American settlers, and hence Art. 2, § 3 of the Constitution of the Republic of Texas gives the congress of the Republic the power "to grant charters of incorporation."

Source: *Vernon's Annotated Constitution of the State of Texas.* Reprinted with permission of Thomson Reuters.

light on the historical context of the time of adoption, and often refer to original documents from that time. References to law review articles and other research references point to commentary on the meaning and intent of the sections. An essential part of the annotations is the Notes of Decisions. These annotations provide summaries (called "headnotes") of the key points of law from cases interpreting the provision. Researchers use these headnotes to identify decisions to be read and understood, in order to inform the court of the relevant cases and to make the best arguments to the court for the client's position. The annotations may also identify the location of provisions

Figure 3-2. Annotations to a Section of the Texas Constitution in *Vernon's*

Historical Notes

Earlier Constitutions:
Const.1845, Art. 7, § 31.

Const.1861, Art. 7, § 31.
Const.1866, Art. 7, § 30.

Cross References

Corporations, statutory provisions, see V.A.T.S. Bus. Corp. Act, art. 2.01 et seq.

Library References

Corporations ⊙4, 12.
Westlaw Topic No. 101.

C.J.S. Corporations §§ 19 to 23, 25 to 28, 32 to 37, 39 to 44, 559.

Research References

Encyclopedias
TX Jur. 3d Corporations § 36, Rule Precluding Collateral Attack – Application of Rule.

Hamilton, 20 Tex. Prac. Series § 26.4, The Corporation as a "Grant" or "Franchise".

Treatises and Practice Aids
Hamilton, 19 Tex. Prac. Series § 1.2, a Look Backward.

Notes of Decisions

In general 1
Special acts 2

―――――

1. In general

Under this section a private corporation can be created only by general laws providing therefor. G.C. Ry. Co. v. G.C.S. Ry. Co. (1885) 63 Tex. 529.

Our constitution provides that corporations shall be created only be general laws and it would seem that one purpose of the provision was to prevent the Legislature from granting to one corporation special powers or special privi-

leges. At all events, the general law should be construed as a general rule conferring upon each member of each particular class of corporations precisely the same powers. North Side Ry. Co. v. Worthington (Sup. 1895) 88 Tex. 562, 30 S.W. 1055, 53 Am.St.Rep. 778.

State held to have right to question right to exercise corporation's franchise originally granted by it. State v. Dilbeck (Civ.App. 1927) 297 S.W. 1049, error refused, certiorari denied 48 S.Ct. 339, 276 U.S. 633, 72 L.Ed. 742. Insurance ⊙ 1162

Powers, franchises, and privileges of corporation are derived exclusively from Constitution and statutes. Marchman v. McCoy Hotel Oper-

425

Source: *Vernon's Annotated Constitution of the State of Texas.* Reprinted with permission of Thomson Reuters.

with the same language in earlier constitutions, indicating that case law from those periods may be referred to when interpreting the provision in the current constitution.

IV. Other Resources for Texas Constitutional Research

Constitutional law consists to a great degree of the interpretations of the language of a constitution by the courts. The long histories of interpretation through many cases can make understanding the current interpretation very difficult. Constitutional law is a subject of study by experts who devote much effort to synthesizing the case law and explaining the current status of constitutional law. A good practice is to start research in any new and complex subject in secondary authorities, such as the more authoritative treatises. It is particularly important to begin research in secondary authority when researching constitutional law. Since Texas constitutional law is not the subject of recent treatises,[5] research should begin with a study of other commentary, such as law review articles, *Texas Jurisprudence, 3d* chapters, or A.L.R. annotations.[6] The annotations in *Vernon's* provide references to these sources for each section of the constitution. The interpretive commentary found after some constitutional sections in *Vernon's* can also be very useful.

V. Updating Texas Constitutional Research

While many constitutions change rarely, the Constitution of the State of Texas is frequently amended. Article XVII of the constitution states that an amendment to the constitution must be approved by a two-thirds vote of each chamber of the legislature, then submitted to the electorate as a proposition. A vote in favor by a majority of the votes cast is sufficient to make the amendment part of the constitution.[7]

Thus, research on the constitution is somewhat similar to statutory research, with techniques for tracking developments in the legislature and making sure you have the most current text of the constitution. When using an annotated code, such as the *Vernon's* set, check the "pocket part," a supplement updating the material in a volume, at the back of each volume.[8] The pocket part is important for

---

5. A somewhat dated, but still useful work, is Janice C. May, *The Texas State Constitution: A Reference Guide* (Greenwood Press 1996). Reprinted as *The Texas State Constitution* (Oxford University Press 2011).

6. Chapter 10 of this book discusses these secondary resources.

7. Tex. Const. art. XVII, § 1.

8. Sometimes the supplementation is too bulky to fit into the volume as a pocket part. In that case, the supplementation will be supplied as a separate paperback pamphlet to be shelved immediately following the main vol-

finding changes in the language of a constitutional section, for locating citations to new cases, and for updating other research references subsequent to the publication of the main volume. Of course, the pocket parts are not completely up to date, since they are published annually and there is a significant lag between collection of information by the publishers and arrival of the pocket part on the shelves of the library. Other tools are needed to bring the research more current. To look for more recent cases, check the "advance sheets"—paperback volumes intended to get new cases to the shelves quickly—to the *South Western Reporter, 3d Series* or *Texas Cases.*[9]

Recent updates to the constitution can be tracked with the *Vernon's Texas Session Law Service* to the *Vernon's* set, which is shelved with the *Vernon's* set and appears frequently in paperback during a legislative session to publish quickly the text of new public laws and constitutional amendments. As well-developed as such tools are, they cannot be kept as current as can online legal research tools. Even the researcher who prefers to begin research in the print formats, and there are often good reasons for using the print, must now use electronic tools to be certain of finding the most current authority.

VI. Researching Constitutional Law Online

A. Westlaw and LexisNexis

Westlaw and LexisNexis have annotated and unannotated versions of the Constitution of the State of Texas. Although these online versions can be searched using the techniques discussed in Chapter 2, the relevant sections of the constitution will likely have been identified from preliminary reading in secondary sources.

---

ume. If you cannot find a pocket part, look to see if there is a separate supplemental pamphlet.

9. The *South Western Reporter, 3d Series* and *South Western Reporter, 3d Series (Texas Cases)* are the publications in which the decisions of the Texas appellate courts appear in print. They are discussed in greater depth in Chapter 4.

The Westlaw annotated version of the Texas Constitution online is very similar to the *Vernon's* print version in organization and appearance, although enhanced by hyperlinks for ease of navigation within the annotations. Westlaw also contains many of the research resources mentioned in the earlier discussion of the annotations, making it easy to navigate to and use those resources during the same online session. The online version has the further advantage of being more current than the print version, both as to the text of the constitution and the case headnotes and other annotations. Be sure to check the date to which the section has been brought current. In Westlaw, this is done by clicking on the link "Currentness."

The LexisNexis annotated version is much less complete, containing only links to case reports from some sections, but not all. Unlike West, LexisNexis does not publish an annotated Texas constitution or annotated Texas statutes in print. LexisNexis has added some case annotations, but the researcher using only LexisNexis will need to supplement the annotations by searching the case law and secondary authority interpreting the Texas constitution by using techniques discussed in Chapters 5 and 10. In LexisNexis, a note above the title of the section tells how current the text of the document is and how current the annotations are.

While the legislature is in session, even the online texts of the documents may not be current. It may be necessary to use legislative updating techniques discussed in Chapter 7 to be sure of capturing the most recent developments.

B. Texas State Legislature Website

The Constitution of the State of Texas is available from the web page of the Texas Legislature.[10] This database of the constitution may be searched by full-text searching techniques, and by a table of contents. The page also contains a note of the most recent changes made to the constitution by amendments; in February 2012, the database

---

10. The address is www.constitution.legis.state.tx.us.

had been updated to include amendments made to the constitution in 2009.

VII. Interpreting the Texas Constitution

In constitutional law research, as in statutory research (Chapter 6), do not stop at reading the plain language of the constitution. In fact, much litigation turns on just what those words mean. The court may need to interpret the meaning of the words in order to formulate the rule to be used to decide a particular dispute. Counsel for each side will attempt to argue for interpretations most favorable to their client's position. Their research will be directed to developing from various sorts of authority and evidence the arguments that the judges may accept as guides to proper interpretation of the meaning of the words of the section. The court will look to various factors. The Supreme Court of Texas has stated:

> When interpreting our state Constitution, we rely heavily on its literal text, and are to give effect to its plain language. We also may consider such things as the purpose of the constitutional provision, the historical context in which it was written, the collective intent, if it can be ascertained, of the framers and the people who adopted it, our prior judicial decisions, the interpretations of analogous constitutional provisions by other jurisdictions, and constitutional theory.[11]

The Supreme Court of Texas has succinctly summarized in this quote the things a court will look to when interpreting the language of a constitution. A court will look first to the text and its "plain language," but that language is often not clear in its application to a particular set of facts. The court may inquire as to the purpose of the provision and the intent of the drafters and those who adopted it. Documents from the record of the constitutional deliberations or the history and debates of the time, or of the legislative actions and de-

---

11. *Republican Party of Texas v. Dietz*, 940 S.W.2d 86, 89 (Tex. 1997) (citations omitted).

bates leading to the amendments, might be examined to shed light on intent.[12] If the court has previously decided cases interpreting the meaning of the section, the opinions will be looked to for guidance (the inferior courts must accept any decisions on the matter by the Supreme Court as mandatory authority). If these guides to interpretation from within the State of Texas are not sufficient, the court may look to general principles of constitutional theory, as developed by legal scholars, for guidance. Similar resources are looked to by courts in interpreting statutes, as discussed in Chapter 6 on statutory law.

VIII. Texas Constitution or Federal Constitution?

Many rights and privileges of citizens are protected by both the Texas and federal constitutions, but the scope of the protection provided may differ, because of differences either in the original language or in the interpretations by the Texas and United States Supreme Courts. It may thus be more advantageous to bring constitutional claims in the courts of Texas or in the federal courts. The lawyer should carefully consider the constitutional law of both before initiating an action.

IX. Researching the United States Constitution

Much of the discussion about Texas constitutional research applies to federal constitutional research. Unlike the Constitution of the State of Texas, however, the Constitution of the United States is brief. The Constitution of the United States is only about twenty pages long, although the annotated constitution fills many volumes.

Research in federal constitutional law seeks the same types of resources as research in Texas law. Secondary resources in the form of

---

12. This process is similar to the use of legislative history as an aid to statutory construction, discussed in Chapter 7.

expert commentary are essential starting points: identify a leading treatise and use the treatise to become familiar with the issues presented in your project (see Chapter 10 on finding and using secondary authority). Next, locate the relevant parts of the constitution and read carefully. After reading secondary resources and the language of the constitution, locate and study thoroughly the decisions of the Supreme Court of the United States. You may also need to locate and examine historical documents from the time of the foundation of the United States, such as the records and debates of the Constitutional Convention. The annotations to the constitutional sections and amendments, either in West's *United States Code Annotated* (U.S.C.A.) or LexisNexis' *United States Code Service* (U.S.C.S.) are invaluable for locating secondary resources and the judicial opinions necessary for understanding the development of the interpretation of the language of the constitution. Westlaw contains an online version of the U.S.C.A. and LexisNexis contains an online version of the U.S.C.S. The online versions of each annotated code and constitution are generally more current than the paper versions.

The processes of identifying good resources will be further developed in Chapter 10 for secondary authority and in Chapters 4 and 5 for case law.

Chapter 4

Court Systems and Judicial Opinions

I. Opinions, Cases, and Reporters

The published opinions[1] of courts, commonly called "cases," are of great importance in the American legal system. This emphasis reflects the origins of our legal system in the judge-made common law of England, even though much case law now interprets the purpose and meaning of constitutions, statutes, and administrative rules. The importance of judicial opinions as legal authority is evident in the many thousands of volumes containing the printed cases of courts.

Cases are printed in serial publications called "reporters," which may be either government publications or publications by commercial publishers. The commercial publications may or may not have the status of official publications, depending on their recognition by the governments of which the courts are a part. The case reporters published by commercial publishers are usually more useful to the researcher, due to editorial enhancements and their links to extensive legal research systems. These features of commercial case reporters are discussed later in this chapter and in Chapter 5.

Many reporters have existed for well over a century, with titles known to every lawyer. A print reporter must be cited if a case is printed, in spite of the availability of most opinions in electronic for-

---

1. Although the terms "decision" and "opinion" are often used interchangeably, there is a difference. The decision states the outcome of the case (i.e., which party prevails), while the opinion is the court's explanation of the legal rule applied to arrive at the holding of the case.

mats. The publishing company West, now a part of the Thomson Reuters group of companies, has been the predominant publisher of the opinions of American courts since the 1880s, when it began the West National Reporter System (N.R.S.). The N.R.S. publishes opinions from the three levels of the United States federal courts, certain specialized federal courts, and opinions from the courts of all states.

The primary case reporters for the opinions of state case law are the regional reporters. An example is West's *South Western Reporter* in its original series and the subsequent second and third series. The titles of the regional reporters coincide only very roughly with the normal understanding of the geographical areas in the titles. For example, most people are surprised to hear that Oklahoma opinions are included in the *Pacific Reporter* and its later series. The geographical coverage of the regional reporters also does not match that of the federal circuits. For the geographical coverage of the regional reporters, see Table 4-1.

In addition to the regional reporters, West publishes reporters containing just the opinions for a state in the series. Examples are *South Western Reporter, 3d Series (Texas Cases)* and *North Western Reporter, 3d Series (Illinois Decisions)*. West also publishes reporters containing cases from the intermediate appellate courts of California and New York, the *California Reporter* and the *New York Supplement*. The *Pacific Reporter* and *North Eastern Reporter* series include only the reports for the highest appellate courts of California and New York.

II. Court Systems: General

In order to know where to find case law, the researcher must understand the structure of the court system in the relevant jurisdiction. The typical court structure includes a trial court, an intermediate court of appeals, and an ultimate court of appeals, often called the "supreme" court. This structure is found at the federal level and in most states, although some states may lack the intermediate court of appeals or have more than one type of court at any of the levels. Texas

Table 4-1. West Regional Reporters and States Included

Atlantic Reporter (A., A.2d)	Connecticut, Delaware, District of Columbia, Maine, Maryland, New Hampshire, New Jersey, Pennsylvania, Rhode Island, and Vermont
North Eastern Reporter (N.E., N.E.2d)	Illinois, Indiana, Massachusetts, New York, and Ohio
North Western Reporter (N.W., N.W.2d)	Iowa, Michigan, Minnesota, Nebraska, North Dakota, South Dakota, and Wisconsin
Pacific Reporter (P., P.2d, P.3d)	Alaska, Arizona, California, Colorado, Hawaii, Idaho, Kansas, Montana, Nevada, New Mexico, Oklahoma, Oregon, Utah, Washington, and Wyoming
South Eastern Reporter (S.E., S.E.2d)	Georgia, North Carolina, South Carolina, Virginia, and West Virginia
South Western Reporter (S.W., S.W.2d, S.W.3d)	Arkansas, Kentucky, Missouri, Tennessee, and Texas
Southern Reporter (So., So. 2d)	Alabama, Florida, Louisiana, and Mississippi

is one of the states with a variation on the typical structure, as explained in Part III.

III. Texas Court System

The Texas court system has some unusual features, with which the researcher must be familiar in order to search effectively in Texas law. The researcher must also understand something about the history of Texas courts in order to recognize the names of courts and other bodies authorized to decide controversies and issue opinions. These bodies and their names have varied over time, as has the precedential weight of opinions issued by them.

A. The Texas Court System: 1981 to Present

The researcher will be looking for cases from the Supreme Court of Texas, the Texas Court of Criminal Appeals, or the courts of appeals of Texas. The trial courts do not issue opinions.

1. Supreme Court of Texas and Texas Court of Criminal Appeals

Texas is unusual in having two ultimate appellate courts, one for civil matters and one for criminal matters. The Supreme Court of Texas is the ultimate appellate court for most civil and juvenile matters. The Texas Supreme Court consists of eight Justices and a Chief Justice, elected for six-year, overlapping terms. The Texas Court of Criminal Appeals is the ultimate appellate court for criminal matters. Appeals to the Court of Criminal Appeals are from the courts of appeals (discussed in Section 2), except that all death penalty cases go directly to the Court of Criminal Appeals from the trial court. The Court of Criminal Appeals consists of eight Associate Judges and a Presiding Judge, also elected for overlapping six-year terms.

The decisions and opinions of the Supreme Court of Texas and the Court of Criminal Appeals are published in West's *South Western Reporter*, now in its third series. The publication of Texas court opinions by the government ended in 1962, when the publication of *Texas Reports*, the official reporter for the Supreme Court of Texas, and *Texas Criminal Reports*, the official reporter for the Court of Criminal Appeals, ceased.

2. Courts of Appeals of Texas

The courts of appeals of Texas hear appeals in both civil and criminal matters from trial courts. The history of intermediate appellate

Table 4-2. Locations of Texas Courts of Appeals

District	City
District 1	Houston
District 2	Fort Worth
District 3	Austin
District 4	San Antonio
District 5	Dallas
District 6	Texarkana
District 7	Amarillo
District 8	El Paso
District 9	Beaumont
District 10	Waco
District 11	Eastland
District 12	Tyler
District 13	Corpus Christi & Edinburg
District 14	Houston

courts in Texas is complex; a brief history is given later in this chapter. The courts of appeals are organized into fourteen districts, each with several Justices. Each district is named by its number and the title "Court of Appeals of Texas"; for example, the Second Court of Appeals of Texas. See Table 4-2 for the location of the fourteen districts. The decisions and opinions of the courts of appeals are published in West's *South Western Reporter*, now in its third series. As discussed further in Appendix A, a citation to a court of appeals decision must include the location of the court issuing the decision. A striking peculiarity of case law research in Texas is that the subsequent history of any order or decision appealed to the Supreme Court of Texas or Court of Criminal Appeals must be included in the citation. This complex subject is discussed in detail in Part XII. of this chapter and in Appendix A, Legal Citation.

3. Trial Courts

The trial courts include: district courts; criminal district courts, in some populous areas; constitutional county courts; statutory county courts at law;[2] probate courts; plus two types of local courts with limited jurisdiction, the justice of the peace courts and the municipal courts. Practitioners must become familiar with the courts in their area and their particular subject matter and jurisdictional amount limits. *The American Bench*, published annually, includes information about the Texas courts. Links to the courts can be found from the official court web portal, at www.courts.state.tx.us.

4. Appointment of Judges and Justices

Judges and justices in Texas are elected officials, as required by the Constitution of the State of Texas.[3] The governor fills vacancies in the state courts by appointment lasting until the next general election for state officers and the qualification of the elected successor.[4]

B. Brief History of the Courts of Texas Before 1981

The history of the Texas appellate courts—their changing names and jurisdictions—and the reporters in which their cases were published is complex. This history is reviewed next.

1. Courts of the Republic and Early Statehood: 1836–1876

The Constitution of 1836 provided for a Supreme Court of the Republic of Texas and inferior courts as established by the legislature. The Supreme Court had appellate jurisdiction in civil and criminal matters. The Supreme Court first met in 1840, and wrote 140 opinions before it was dissolved after the 1845 term. The opinions were published only in newspapers at the time, but the opinions for the

---

2. Each county has a constitutional county court. A number of more populous counties have additional courts established by the legislature; these are called county courts at law.

3. Tex. Const. art. V, §§ 2, 4, 6, 7, 15.

4. Tex. Const. art. V, § 28(a).

1840 through 1844 terms were ultimately published in *Dallam's Digest*, which remains the source for locating and citing the cases.[5] The cases of the 1845 term were not published until 1986.[6]

After Texas was admitted to the Union in 1845, the Constitution of 1845 provided for a Supreme Court, district courts, and inferior courts as the legislature established them. The Supreme Court consisted of a Chief Justice and two Associate Justices. It had general appellate jurisdiction, but appeals of criminal matters could be heard only as allowed by the legislature. The cases of the Supreme Court from this period were published in an official case reporter, *Texas Reports*, which was published until 1962.

Upon the secession of Texas from the Union in 1861, the Constitution of 1861 maintained the existing court system in effect. Publication of court opinions ceased during the war, due to the unavailability of paper. The case reports of the Civil War period were ultimately published in volumes 36 and 37 of the *Texas Reports* published in 1867, and the cases of the 1860 term were published in a supplemental volume 35 to the *Texas Reports* in 1869. The Civil War cases are precedential and have been cited by a number of courts inside Texas and outside, including the U.S. Supreme Court.

The Reconstruction period, 1866–1873, saw three successive supreme courts, the opinions of which vary as to precedential value. The decisions of the Presidential Reconstruction Court of 1866–1867, established under the Constitution of 1866, are precedential. The Military Court, also known as the Congressional Reconstruction Court, sat from 1867 to 1870, following the imposition of military rule on Texas. The Supreme Court of Texas has held that the decisions of this

---

5. James W. Dallam, *A Digest of the Laws of Texas: Containing a Full and Complete Compilation of the Land Laws: Together with the Opinions of the Supreme Court From 1840 to 1844 Inclusive* (1845)(called Dallam's Digest). The cases were published at the end of this original publication, and have been reprinted separately subsequently.

6. James W. Paulsen, *The Missing Cases of the Republic*, 65 Tex. L. Rev. 372 (1986).

court are not precedential, since the court operated only under military appointment, rather than under the authority of a constitution of the State of Texas. Opinions of the Military Court are, however, sometimes cited favorably as persuasive authority.

No history of the Texas courts would be complete without a mention of the "Semicolon Court." The Third Reconstruction Court sat from 1870 to 1873. This court, established under the Constitution of 1869, issued as its last opinion the much-denigrated *Ex parte Rodriguez*, in which the court decided the unconstitutionality of the election of 1873 (which affected the composition of the Texas Supreme Court itself) based upon the placement of a semicolon in the 1869 Constitution.[7] The decision was ignored, the election results stood, a new governor was seated, and the court itself was expanded from three to five justices. Although the decisions of the Semicolon Court are technically fully precedential, they are disfavored by lawyers and judges due to the infamy of *Rodriguez*, and citation to them is generally avoided.

2. The Courts from 1876 to 1891

The current constitution, the Constitution of the State of Texas of 1876, made a fundamental change in the structure of Texas courts. The Texas Supreme Court under the 1876 Constitution had appellate jurisdiction only in civil cases appealed from the district courts. A new Texas Court of Appeals had exclusive appellate jurisdiction in criminal cases and also in civil cases appealed from the county courts. The existence of a separate criminal appellate court has continued to this day.

Another unusual feature of the Texas judiciary appeared during this time: appellate commissions aiding and supplementing the work of the highest appellate courts. In 1879, the legislature created a Commission of Appeals (the "Old" Texas Commission of Appeals) to hear

---

7. 39 Tex. 705 (1873).

cases referred to it by the Texas Supreme Court and the Texas Court of Appeals. From 1881 onward, those decisions of the commission that were adopted by the Texas Supreme Court were published in *Texas Reports* and have precedential value as if decided by the Texas Supreme Court. This commission existed until 1892.

3. The Courts from 1892 to 1981

An 1891 amendment to the constitution reconstituted the courts of Texas, with the primary change of interest to the legal researcher being the change of the Texas Court of Appeals to the Texas Court of Criminal Appeals, with exclusively criminal appellate jurisdiction. As part of the reform, the courts of civil appeals of Texas were established, with intermediate appellate jurisdiction in civil matters. Criminal appeals continued to move directly from the trial courts to the Texas Court of Criminal Appeals. The new court system went into effect in 1892.

In 1918, a Commission of Appeals (the "New" Texas Commission of Appeals) was established to assist the supreme court with the burden of civil appeals. When approved by the supreme court, an opinion of the commission was published in *Texas Reports* and in West's *South Western Reporter*[8] and was precedential as if decided by the supreme court itself. This commission continued in existence until 1945, when the supreme court was expanded from three justices to nine.

During part of this period, the Texas Court of Criminal Appeals also was assisted by a commission, the Commission in Aid of the Court of Criminal Appeals. This commission was authorized in 1925 and has been appointed at various times to assist the Court of Criminal Appeals with heavy case loads. An opinion issued by commissioners and approved by the Court of Criminal Appeals is cited as if it were an opinion of the Court of Criminal Appeals. No commissioners have been appointed in recent years.

---

8. West's *South Western Reporter* began publishing Texas cases in 1886.

4. The Courts from 1981 to Present

The most recent change to the court system came in 1981, when the courts of civil appeals of Texas became the courts of appeals of Texas, with intermediate appellate jurisdiction in both civil and criminal matters (except that death penalty appeals go directly to the Texas Court of Criminal Appeals from the trial courts).

The opinions of the Texas Supreme Court, the Texas Court of Criminal Appeals, and the courts of appeals are published in *South Western Reporter, 3d*. Recent opinions of the Texas Supreme Court are also published on the court's website and in the *Texas Supreme Court Journal*. For cases that have not yet appeared in *South Western Reporter, 3d*, you may use a citation to LexisNexis or Westlaw, to the court's website, or to the *Texas Supreme Court Journal*, with a parallel citation to Lexis-Nexis or Westlaw.[9] See Table 4-3 for a summary of the appellate courts, their jurisdictions, and the most widely used sources in which their opinions were reported. The *Greenbook* does not require parallel citation to official Texas case reporters and *South Western Reporter, 3d* in either legal memoranda or court documents, but it provides a citation form to use if local court rules require parallel citations.[10] An exception is that courts of civil appeals cases from 1892 to 1911 must have parallel cites in documents filed with courts.[11]

IV. Court Systems of Other States

The structure of state court systems varies from state to state. The attorney practicing within a state must know the organization and ju-

---

9. Tex. Law Review Ass'n, *The Greenbook: Texas Rules of Form*, Rule 2.1.2, at 6 (12th ed. 2010). The *Greenbook* is the Texas legal citation manual published by the Texas Law Review Association. *Greenbook* citation rules are discussed in Appendix A.

10. *Id.*, R. 2.3.2., at 9, R. 3.3., at 13.

11. *Id.*, R. 4.2.2., at 19.

Table 4-3. Texas Appellate Courts

Date	Court	Jurisdiction	Reporter
1836–1845	Supreme Court	Civil and Criminal	*Dallam's Digest*
1845–1876	Supreme Court*	Civil and Criminal	*Texas Reports*
1876–1892	Supreme Court	Civil	*Texas Reports* *South Western Reporter* (1886–)
	Court of Appeals	Criminal, some Civil	*Texas Court of Appeals* *Reports* (1876–1892)
	"Old" Commission of Appeals (1879–1892)**	Civil	*Texas Reports* (1881–1892) *South Western Reporter* (1886–1892)
1892–1981	Supreme Court	Civil, Highest	*Texas Reports* (to 1962) *South Western Reporter, S.W.2d*
	"New" Commission of Appeals (1918–1945)	Civil	*Texas Reports*
	Court of Criminal Appeals	Criminal	*Texas Criminal Reports* (1892–1962) *South Western Reporter, S.W.2d* (1911–1981)
	Commission in Aid of the Court of Criminal Appeals (1925–Present)***	Criminal	*Texas Criminal Reports* (1925–1962) *South Western Reporter, S.W.2d*
	Courts of civil appeals	Civil, Intermediate	*Texas Civil Appeals Reports* (1892–1911) *South Western Reporter, S.W.2d*
1981–	Supreme Court	Civil, Highest	*South Western Reporter 2d, 3d*
	Court of Criminal Appeals	Criminal, Highest	*South Western Reporter 2d, 3d*
	Courts of appeals	Civil and Criminal, Intermediate	*South Western Reporter 2d, 3d*

* Includes the three Reconstruction Courts, which sat from 1866 to 1873. Civil War conscript cases by the Texas Supreme Court were issued from 1862 to 1865. These are of interest only to legal historians. See Greenbook Appendix A for information about these cases.
** The cases of the commission from 1879 to 1881 were not adopted by the Texas Supreme Court and are considered to be unpublished. Cases referred to the commission by the Texas Court of Appeals were not published. Two private reporters included the unpublished cases of the commission. See Greenbook Appendix C for information about the private reporters.
*** The Court of Criminal Appeals has continuing constitutional and statutory authority to appoint commissioners in aid, but no commissioners have been appointed in recent years.

risdictional assignments of that state's courts. The researcher in the law of an unfamiliar state should consult reference works, such as *The*

American Bench, or the state's court administration's website and publications.

V. United States Federal Court System

The United States court system is a three-tier system. The tiers are: the courts of the United States District Courts, the trial courts; the courts of the United States Courts of Appeals, the intermediate courts of appeals; and the Supreme Court of the United States.

The United States District Courts are organized in ninety-four districts, each of which is contained within a single state. States with small populations might have only one district, while very populous states are divided into several districts. Texas has four districts: the Eastern District, headquartered in Tyler; the Northern District, headquartered in Dallas; the Western District, headquartered in San Antonio; and the Southern District, headquartered in Houston. Each of the districts contains six or seven divisions, sitting in different towns within the district. Each district also contains within it a bankruptcy court, a specialized court operating under the district court's jurisdiction.

The thirteen circuits of the United States Courts of Appeals are organized in twelve geographical regions, including the District of Columbia Circuit, plus the Federal Circuit. The courts of the twelve geographical circuits hear appeals from the district courts within the states of their circuit. The thirteenth court, the Federal Circuit Court, hears appeals from all the other circuits on patent law cases, as well as appeals from certain specialized courts. Texas is located in the Fifth Circuit, which hears appeals from the district courts in Texas, Louisiana, and Mississippi.

The Supreme Court of the United States is the ultimate appellate court in the federal court system. It hears appeals from cases decided by the circuit courts, as well as certain cases that may constitutionally be appealed from the supreme courts of the states. The appellate jurisdiction of the Supreme Court of the United States is discretionary, with the court choosing whether to grant or deny appeals made by writ of certiorari. The Supreme Court consists of eight Associate Justices and a Chief Justice. Supreme Court justices are appointed for life.[12]

VI. Reporters for Texas Cases

Over the long history of the Texas courts, their opinions have been published in a variety of reporters, both official and unofficial. The reporters most frequently needed by the researcher in Texas law are the three series of West's *South Western Reporter* (1886–present), the official *Texas Reports* (1846–1962), and the official *Texas Criminal Reports* (1892–1962). The researcher might also use the *Texas Cases* set for convenient access to the Texas opinions from the *South Western Reporter* series. The opinions of the commissions discussed above were published in these and other reporters whenever the Texas Supreme Court or the Court of Criminal Appeals adopted the opinions as if they were their own.

The opinions of Texas courts have been published in different reporters at different times. Part II of the *Greenbook*, and Table T.1 of the *Bluebook*[13] include the titles of the Texas case reporters, the years they cover, and the preferred reporter for citation. It is important to note that the *Greenbook* requires citation to the official reporter for the court if the case appears in it, while the *Bluebook* rule is that ci-

---

12. Under Article III of the United States Constitution, judges of the United States courts "hold their offices during good Behaviour." The exception is bankruptcy judges, who are not Article III judges. Bankruptcy judges are appointed to terms of fourteen years.

13. *The Bluebook: A Uniform System of Citation* (Columbia Law Review Ass'n et al. eds., 19th ed. 2010). The *Bluebook* is the legal citation manual compiled by the editors of the Columbia Law Review, the Harvard Law Review, the University of Pennsylvania Law Review, and the Yale Law Journal. Long the predominant guide to American legal citation practice, it now shares the field with the *ALWD Citation Manual*. The *Greenbook* establishes the *Bluebook* as the authoritative citation guide in Texas, except where the rules of the *Greenbook* differ from those of the *Bluebook*. The *Bluebook*, *Greenbook*, and *ALWD* citation manuals are discussed in Appendix A.

tation should be to the *South Western Reporter* or its second or third series, if the case appears in it. The *Greenbook* rule prevails over the *Bluebook* rule for the legal researcher working in Texas, where access to the official reporters is widespread. The *Bluebook* rule may be applied outside Texas, where the researcher is likely to have access only to the *South Western Reporter* series. The *Greenbook* and the *Bluebook* also contain useful historical information about publications and tips for the researcher. Table 4-3 summarizes the coverage of the most widely used sources for Texas case law.

VII. Reporters for Federal Cases

A. United States Supreme Court

All opinions and decisions of the United States Supreme Court are published. The opinions of the United States Supreme Court are published in an official reporter, *United States Reports*, and two unofficial commercial reporters, West's *Supreme Court Reporter* and *United States Reports: Lawyers' Edition* (Lexis® Law Publishing), commonly known as the *Lawyers' Edition*. The researcher will usually use one of the commercial reporters. They are published more currently than the *United States Reports*, and they contain enhancements allowing them to be used together with the other publications by their publishers.

The *Supreme Court Reporter*, as with the other reporters in the West National Reporter System, has abstracts of the points of law in each case. These editor-written "headnotes" form the basis of the American Digest System, a powerful case-finding tool. The American Digest System is discussed in detail in Chapter 5.

The *Lawyers' Edition* also adds abstracts to the cases, but these abstracts are less useful, because they are gathered only in the digest to the *Lawyer's Edition*. The *Lawyers' Edition* does, however, include some enhancements not found in the *Supreme Court Reporter*. The *Lawyers' Edition* contains summaries of the briefs submitted in the cases reported and the names of counsel on the briefs. Also supplied are analyses, called "annotations," exploring at length the status of legal issues of selected cases reported in each volume.

B. United States Courts of Appeals and United States District Courts

Opinions of the circuit courts of appeals are published in West's *Federal Reporter*, now in its third series. Opinions of the district courts are published in West's *Federal Supplement*, now in its second series. There are no official reporters for the U.S. Courts of Appeals or the U.S. District Courts.

C. Special Courts and Topics

Reporters also exist to gather the cases on certain topics or from specialized courts. For example, West's *Bankruptcy Reporter* publishes many cases from the bankruptcy courts, which, as arms of the federal districts, are trial level courts. Many of these cases are not published in other reporters of federal cases. Similarly, West's *Federal Rules Decisions* publishes cases from the federal trial courts interpreting federal rules of procedure. Other specialized reporters include West's *Military Justice Reporter*, the independently published *American Maritime Cases*, and publications by the federal government, such as *Reports of the United States Tax Court.*

VIII. Unpublished Opinions

Not all court opinions are published. Only about twenty percent of the opinions of the U.S. Courts of Appeals are published[14] and a tiny percentage of the decisions of the U.S. District Courts are pub-

---

14. Admin. Off. of U.S. Cts., *Judicial Facts and Figures 2006, Table 2-5,* www.uscourts.gov/uscourts/Statistics/JudicialFactsandFigures/2006/Table205.pdf.

lished. The rest of the decisions are "unpublished." It may seem strange that so many decisions of the courts are unpublished. Even more surprising is that many unpublished opinions of the federal courts are available in Westlaw or LexisNexis, or even actually in print in a West reporter series, West's *Federal Appendix.*

An unpublished opinion is an opinion that was not approved by the issuing judge for publication in the *Federal Reporter* or *Federal Supplement* reporter series. For many years, this determination meant the cases could not be cited to the courts as precedent. The practice of not approving cases for publication began in the 1960s as an effort by court administrators to reduce the workload on judges and to reduce a perceived excess of published opinions that had no significant effect on established law. The practice of not approving cases for publication was adopted by many state court systems, as well. In Texas, only about fifteen percent of the decisions of the fourteen courts of appeals were published in 2000.[15]

The practice of not approving cases for publication became increasingly controversial, with the result that the U.S. Supreme Court issued in 2006 a new rule of appellate procedure stating that "a court may not prohibit or restrict" the citation of unpublished cases issued on or after January 1, 2007.[16] The rule does not dictate the precedential value to be given to unpublished cases. The precedential value varies according to the rules adopted by each circuit.

In 2002, the Texas Supreme Court changed the rules on unpublished opinions (with revisions in 2008). Rule 47 of the Texas Rules of Civil Procedure now provides that only opinions by the courts of appeals in criminal cases can receive the designation of "do not publish."[17] In civil and criminal cases, the court must designate an opinion as either an "Opinion" or a "Memorandum Opinion."[18] Opinions are to be designated "Memorandum

---

15. Off. of Ct. Admin., *Analysis of Activity for the Year Ended August 31, 2000,* at 2, www.courts.state.tx.us/pubs/AR2000/COA/COANAR00.pdf.

16. Fed. R. App. P. 32.1, 28 U.S.C.A. (West 2005 & Supp. 2011).

17. Tex. R. App. P. 47.2(b), (c) (West 2003 & Supp. 2011).

18. Tex. R. App. P. 47.2(a) (West 2003 & Supp. 2011).

Opinions" if the court determines the case involves no unsettled legal issues, in which case the memorandum opinion is to be very brief.[19] Rule 47 also provides:

> An opinion must be designated a memorandum opinion unless it does any of the following:
> (a) establishes a new rule of law, alters or modifies an existing rule, or applies an existing rule to a novel fact situation likely to recur in future cases;
> (b) involves issues of constitutional law or other legal issues important to the jurisprudence of Texas;
> (c) criticizes existing law; or
> (d) resolves an apparent conflict of authority.[20]

Thus, in civil cases, the memorandum opinion is published. Published memorandum opinions, civil or criminal, are brief and are understood to have little precedential value. In criminal cases, some opinions will continue to be designated as unpublished. Under the 2002 rules and 2008 revisions, unpublished opinions may be cited to the courts, with the required notation "(not designated for publication)," but unpublished opinions issued under either the current or prior rules have no precedential value.[21]

How might a lawyer use unpublished opinions? Although the courts themselves may have determined that certain cases break no new ground and should be unpublished, the practitioner might find them useful in predicting how the court will treat a particular matter and might also determine that different courts tend to reach different results in similar cases. These predictions as to how the courts actually decide are the essence of the lawyer's craft. Further, the attorney may use unpublished cases to inform or remind the courts of the decisions reached by them or their sister courts in similar cases. The courts may even, recognizing they are not bound by the cases, be persuaded or supported in reaching a decision by the pattern of previ-

---

19. Tex. R. App. P. 47.4 (West 2003).
20. Tex. R. App. P. 47.4 (West 2003).
21. Tex. R. App. P. 47.7 (West 2003 & Supp. 2011).

ous decisions as revealed by citation of unpublished opinions.[22] The lawyer will want to carefully consider how the court will respond to citation of unpublished opinions and follow exactly any rules for proper submission and citation.

IX. Parts of a Published Judicial Opinion

Familiarity with the information provided in reported cases, whether published in print or electronic databases, leads to more efficient research. The layout of the information provided is very similar in the various case reporters the researcher will be using, although the order of some items may vary. Figure 4-1 shows the first page of a typical reported case. This case is printed in the *South Western Reporter, 3d*, but the same features will be found in any West reporter. Working from the top of the page down, observe the following features.

Citation: At the top of the page is a shortened form of the case name and directions as to how the case is to be cited.[23]

Case Name: The report begins with the full name of the case. The researcher will generally not use this full form when citing to the case, but will apply rules from the *Bluebook* or other citation standards. The first party named in the sample case is the "appellant." This term is used when the losing party filing the appeal has the right to appeal. Next is the abbreviation "v." for versus. Then comes the name of the "appellee," the party prevailing on the order or judgment that is the subject of the appeal.[24]

---

22. *See, e.g., State v. Mechler*, 123 S.W.3d 449, 453 (Tex. App.—Houston [14th Dist.] 2003), *aff'd*, 153 S.W.3d 435 (Tex. Crim. App. 2005).

23. Use these suggested citations with caution. The suggestions are not always totally consistent with *Greenbook* or *Bluebook* form. You may also be working in a jurisdiction or for an employer with their own citation standards.

24. The terms defined here are used in Texas and many other states. Some states use other terms, however, so the researcher should be aware of the terms in use in the jurisdiction being researched.

Figure 4-1. Parts of a Published Opinion

LITTLETON v. PRANGE   Tex. **223**
Cite as 9 S.W.3d 223 (Tex.App.—San Antonio 1999)

**Christie Lee LITTLETON, Individually
and as Next Heir of Jonathon Mark
Littleton, Appellant,**

v.

Dr. Mark PRANGE, Appellee.

No. 04-99-00010-CV.

Court of Appeals of Texas,
San Antonio.

Oct. 27, 1999.

Transsexual, who was born a man but underwent sex reassignment surgery, brought medical malpractice action under Wrongful Death and Survival Statute, in her capacity as surviving spouse of a male patient. The 288th Judicial District Court, Bexar County, Frank Montalvo, J., entered summary judgment for doctor. Transsexual appealed. The Court of Appeals, Hardberger, C.J., held as a matter of first impression that ceremonial marriage between a man and a transsexual born as a man, but surgically and chemically altered to have the physical characteristics of a woman, was not valid, and thus, transsexual lacked standing to bring claim as man's surviving spouse under wrongful death and survival statutes.

Affirmed.

Angelini, J., filed concurring opinion.

Lopez, J., filed dissenting opinion.

1. Husband and Wife ⬡209(4)
   Marriage ⬡54
   Ceremonial marriage between a man and a transsexual born as a man, but surgically and chemically altered to have the physical characteristics of a woman, was not valid, and thus, transsexual lacked standing as man's surviving spouse to bring claim under wrongful death and survival statutes, even though transsexual and man were married for seven years, and she officially changed her birth certificate to reflect her altered status as a woman.

V.T.C.A., Family Code § 2.001(b); V.T.C.A., Health & Safety Code § 191.028; V.T.C.A., Civil Practice & Remedies Code §§ 71.004, 71.021; KRS 402.020(1)(d).

2. Appeal and Error ⬡863
   In an appeal from a summary judgment, the appellate court must determine whether the movant has shown that no genuine issue of material facts exists and that the movant is entitled to judgment as a matter of law.

3. Judgment ⬡185(2)
   In determining whether a material fact issue exists to preclude summary judgment, evidence favoring the nonmovant is taken as true, and all reasonable inferences are indulged in favor of the nonmovant; any doubt is resolved in the nonmovant's favor.

4. Health and Environment ⬡34
   Term "inaccurate" in statute permitting amendment to birth certificate if proved by satisfactory evidence to be inaccurate means inaccurate as of the time the certificate was recorded, that is, at the time of birth. V.T.C.A., Health & Safety Code § 191.028.

Dale Hicks, Jon A. Hyde, Maloney & Maloney, P.C., San Antonio, for Appellant.

Thomas F. Nye, Linda C. Breck, Brin & Brin, P.C., Corpus Christi, for Appellee.

Sitting: PHIL HARDBERGER, Chief Justice, ALMA L. LÓPEZ, Justice, KAREN ANGELINI, Justice.

OPINION

Opinion by: PHIL HARDBERGER, Chief Justice.

This case involves the most basic of questions. When is a man a man, and when is a woman a woman? Every schoolchild, even of tender years, is confident he or she can tell the difference, especially if the person is wearing no clothes. These

Source: *South Western Reporter, Third Series.* Reprinted with permission of Thomson Reuters.

When the losing party must petition the court above to accept the appeal, the term used is "petitioner" and the opposing party is termed the "respondent." Thus, in opinions resulting from appeals to the Supreme Court of Texas or the Supreme Court of the United States, where the courts have discretion in accepting appeals, the parties will be called petitioner and respondent.[25]

Docket Number: Immediately below the case name is the docket number for the case in the court issuing the opinion. The docket number is assigned by the clerk of the court when the case is filed with the court. All documents relating to the case will be assigned this number. The docket number is essential if the researcher needs to review the case file or obtain from the clerk of the court copies of particular documents, such as briefs filed in the case. The docket number is used only for documents and records produced while the case is before the court. When a case is appealed to a higher court, that court will assign its own docket number to the case.

Court: Next in this case report is the name of the court in which the case was decided.

Dates: In the case shown, the heading includes the date on which the case was decided by the court. Sometimes included are dates on which the case was argued, the date on which rehearing was denied, and other dates. For citation purposes, only the year of the decision is needed.

Synopsis: Next is a summary, called the "synopsis," of the case. The synopsis in this case was written by a West editor. In some official reporters, the synopsis is written by an official of the court. The synopsis typically gives a brief summary of the facts, the nature of the claim, the procedural stages in the history of the case, and the decision by the court. If the opinion has a named author, that judge or

---

25. In the titles of cases at the trial court level, the parties will most commonly be called "plaintiff" and "defendant" and their names will appear in that order. The researcher will most commonly encounter these terms in those federal district court cases printed in the *Federal Supplement*. Trial courts in Texas do not publish opinions.

justice is identified, along with the names of any judges or justices issuing dissenting or concurring opinions. If the opinion is by the court as a whole, with no identified author, it is labeled a "per curiam" opinion. Many appellate court cases are decided by a panel of judges, typically three, drawn from the judges or justices of the court. If the case was decided by a panel, that will be noted.

Headnotes: The case in Figure 4-1 is a case from a West N.R.S. reporter. All reporters in the N.R.S. system add to each published case brief abstracts of points of law from the case. These abstracts, called "headnotes," are prepared by West editors. The headnotes may be simple quotes from the case, or they may have been written by the West editor for the case. Each of these headnotes is then assigned a topic and key number from West's Key Number System, which classifies all of American law into over 400 broad topics, which are then divided into subtopics identified by key numbers. Chapter 5 discusses in detail the Key Number System and how it is used in West's digests as a powerful case-finding tool. Note that each headnote is numbered. The number of this headnote is printed in bracketed, bold face type at the point in the opinion at which discussion of that point begins.

Attorneys: Following the headnotes is a section identifying the attorneys for the parties. This feature can be particularly useful in online searching, where a search by attorney name can pull together all the cases in which particular attorneys or firms were involved. This is potentially very useful information to those seeking counsel or assessing the counsel of the opposing side.

Opinion: The opinion is preceded by an identification of the judge or justice who wrote the opinion for the court, as well as the judges or justices joining in the opinion. The text of the opinion typically begins with an introduction containing the court's summary of the facts, the procedural posture of the case, the questions presented, and the decision of the court. The analysis of the issues follows. The "holding" is the answer to the legal question presented to the court, while the "decision" is the procedural result, such as "affirmed," "reversed," or "review denied." The reasoning of the court leading to the decision is called the "*ratio decidendi*."

X. Advance Sheets

The publication of permanent reporter volumes may take several months from the time the opinions issue from the courts. In order to get new opinions to researchers faster, the publishers produce paperback "advance sheets." The cases printed in the advance sheets have the page numbers they will have in the bound reporters, allowing correct citation.

Lawyers and scholars often use the advance sheets to keep current on recent cases and other current developments. For this reason, the publishers include in the advance sheets a number of current awareness features. For example, each advance sheet for *Texas Cases* includes a "Texas Subsequent History Table," which supplements the most recently published annual *Texas Subsequent History Table*. See Part XII.B. in this chapter, explaining this very important feature of Texas case law research and analysis. The advance sheet also contains "Judicial Highlights" of selected decisions from around the nation; a list of Texas cases recently reported in the *South Western Reporter, 3d*; recent orders from the Supreme Court of Texas and the Texas Court of Criminal Appeals; a list of "Words and Phrases" construed in cases contained in the advance sheet; a "Key Number Digest," with headnotes from cases in the advance sheet, organized by topic and key number; and notes of recent changes to court rules in Texas. Certain of these features of advance sheets make them an integral part of the updating process of case research, when the researcher is working in printed reporters. This updating process will be discussed in Chapter 5.

XI. Reading and Analyzing Cases[26]

After locating a case, the researcher must read it, understand it, and analyze its potential relevance to the client's problem. This

---

26. Part XI is borrowed in its entirety, with changes to reflect Texas practice, from Suzanne E. Rowe, *Oregon Legal Research*, 53–58 (2d ed. 2007).

process may take more mental work than you have ever dedicated to just a few pages of text. It is not unusual for a lawyer to spend hours reading and re-reading a complex case. For a novice, this reading is frequently interrupted by referring to a law dictionary to try to understand the terms used.

To aid your early efforts at reading cases, the following sections explain basic concepts of civil procedure and case analysis. The chapter ends with strategies for reading cases effectively.

A. A Thimbleful of Civil Procedure

In Texas, the person who believes he was harmed begins civil litigation by filing an "original petition" in the court he selects. In most states, the pleading beginning civil litigation is called a "complaint." The "plaintiff" is the person who files the original petition; the person against whom the original petition is filed is the "defendant." Courts vary considerably in how much information is required at this stage of the litigation. In Texas, the original petition should give fair notice of the facts relied on, enabling the defendant to prepare a defense.

The defendant has a limited amount of time in which to file a response to the original petition. If the defendant does nothing within the prescribed time, the plaintiff can ask the court for a "default judgment," which would grant the plaintiff the relief sought in the original petition. One form of response to the original petition is the "answer." In Texas, the answer typically takes the form of a general denial; certain denials require additional verification by affidavit based on personal knowledge. The defendant may also raise affirmative defenses and assert claims against the plaintiff.

Throughout the litigation, parties submit a variety of papers to the court for its consideration. Some require no action or response from the court, for example, the filing of the original petition. In other instances, a party asks the court to make a decision or take action. An example is a motion for summary judgment, where a party asks a court to decide in that party's favor without the need for a trial.

When the trial judge grants a motion that ends a case, the losing party can appeal. The appealing party is called the "appellant"; the other party is the "appellee." In deciding an appeal from an order granting a motion, the appellate court is deciding whether the trial judge was correct in issuing the order at that stage of the litigation. If the appellate court agrees with the decision of the trial judge, it will "affirm." If not, the court will "reverse" the order granting the motion and in some instances "remand" the case back to the trial court.

Even at trial, the parties might make motions that can be appealed. For example, during the trial, the plaintiff presents his evidence first. After all of the plaintiff's witnesses have testified, the defendant may move for a "judgment as a matter of law," arguing that the plaintiff cannot win based on the evidence presented and asking for an immediate decision. An order granting that motion could be appealed.

Most reported cases are appeals of orders granting motions. These cases apply different standards of review, depending on the motion that is the object of the appeal. While standards of review are beyond the scope of this book, understanding the procedural posture of the case is crucial to understanding the court's holding. The relevant rules of civil procedure will guide your analysis. Texts listed in Appendix B of this book contain helpful explanations as well.

B. Analyzing the Substance of Cases

Early in your career it may be difficult to determine whether a case is relevant to your research problem. If the case concerns the same legally significant facts as your client's situation and the court applies law on point for your problem, then the case is relevant. Legally significant facts are those that affect the court's decision. Some attorneys call these outcome-determinative facts or key facts. Which facts are legally significant depends on the case. The height of the defendant in a contract dispute is unlikely to be legally significant, but that fact may be critical in a criminal case where the only eye witness testified that the thief was about five feet tall.

Rarely will research reveal a case with facts that are exactly the same as the client's situation. Rather, several cases may involve facts that are similar to your client's situation but not exactly the same. Your job is to determine whether the facts are similar enough for a court to apply the law in the same way and reach the same outcome. If the court reached a decision favorable to your client, highlight the similarities. If, on the other hand, the court reached an unfavorable decision from your client's perspective, you may argue that the case is distinguishable from yours based on its facts or that its reasoning is faulty. You have an ethical duty to ensure that the court knows about a case directly on point, even if the outcome of that case is adverse to your client. It is also unlikely that one case will address all aspects of a client's situation. Most legal claims have several elements or factors. "Elements" are required subparts of a claim, while "factors" are important aspects but not required. If a court decides that one element is not met, it may not discuss others. In a different case, the court may decide that two factors are so overwhelming that others have no impact on the outcome. In these circumstances, you would need to find other cases that analyze the other elements or factors.

Once you determine that a case is relevant to some portion of your analysis, you must decide how heavily it will weigh in your analysis. Two important points need to be considered here. One is the concept of *stare decisis*. The other is the difference between the holding of the case and dicta within that case.

Stare decisis means to "stand by things decided."[27] This means that courts must follow prior opinions, ensuring consistency in the application of the law. This requirement, however, is limited to the courts within one jurisdiction. A Texas court of appeals must follow the decisions of the Texas Supreme Court, but not those of the courts of any other state. The concept of *stare decisis* also refers to a court with respect to its own opinions. A Texas court of appeals, thus, should follow its own earlier cases in deciding new matters. A court may, however, decide not to continue following its earlier cases because of

27. *Black's Law Dictionary* 1442 (8th ed. 2004).

changes in society that have outdated the law, or because a new statute has been enacted that changes the legal landscape.

Under *stare decisis*, courts are required to follow the holding of prior cases. The "holding" is the court's ultimate decision on the matter of law at issue in the case. Other statements or observations are "dicta." For example, a court in a property dispute may hold that the land belongs to Martinez. In reaching that decision, the court may note that had the facts been slightly different, it would have decided the land belonged to Seifer. That observation is not binding on future courts. Dicta may, however, be valuable as an indicator of what the court thinks the law is or should be; the researcher should consider dicta as possibly predictive of what the court may do in cases in which the outcome may turn on those interpretations.

After finding a number of cases that have similar facts, that discuss the same legal issue, and that are binding on the client, the next step is to synthesize the cases to state and explain the legal rule. Sometimes a court states the rule fully; if not, piece together the information from the relevant cases to state the rule completely but concisely. Then use the analysis and facts of various cases to explain the law. Decide how the rule applies to the client's facts, and determine your conclusion. Note that this method of synthesis is much more than mere summaries of all the various cases. Legal analysis texts in Appendix B of this book explain synthesis in detail.

C. Strategies for Reading Cases

The following strategies may help the new researcher understand cases more quickly and more thoroughly.

- Review the synopsis quickly to determine whether the case seems to be on point. If so, skim the headnotes to find the particular portion of the case that is relevant. Remember that one case may discuss several issues of law, only one or two of which may be of interest to you. Go to the portion of the case identified by the relevant headnote and decide whether it is important for your project.

- If so, skim the entire case to get a feeling for what happened and why, focusing on the portion of the case identified by the relevant headnote.

- Read the case slowly and carefully. Skip the parts that are obviously not pertinent to your problem. For example, when researching a property question, there is no need to scrutinize the tort issue that is not pertinent to your property question.

- At the end of each paragraph or page, consider what you have read. If you cannot summarize it, try reading the material again.

- The next time you read the case, take notes. The notes may be in the form of a formal "case brief" or they may be scribbles that only you can understand. Regardless of the form, the process of taking notes will help you parse through, identify, and comprehend the essential concepts of the case. In law school, the notes will record your understanding of the case both for class discussion and for the end of the semester when you begin to review for exams. When preparing to write a legal document, the notes will assist you in organizing your analysis into an outline.

- Note that skimming text online or highlighting a printed page is often not sufficient to achieve thorough comprehension of judicial opinions.

Often you will read groups of cases as you conduct research. Reading the cases and understanding the law will be easier with an organized approach. First, organize groups of cases according to jurisdiction and then by decision date. Learning how the law developed over time in each jurisdiction will be easier if you read the cases chronologically. Finding the current rule of law will likely be easier if you begin with the most recent cases. Define your goal and organize the order in which you read the cases accordingly.

Pay attention to how the cases fit together. Look for trends in the law and in the facts of the cases. Has the law remained unchanged or have new elements been introduced? Has the meaning of an important term been redefined? Have certain facts virtually guaranteed success for one party while other facts have tended to cause difficulties?

Does one case summarize the current rule or do you have to synthesize a rule from several cases that each address part of the rule?

XII. Precedential Value of Texas Cases: Subsequent History

A. Subsequent History Notation: General

The *Bluebook* requires that case citations include subsequent history notations for cases appealed to higher courts. An example of subsequent history notation is "aff'd", for a judgment that is affirmed after review on the merits by the higher court. These signals, as well as notations for some prior history, indicate the weight of authority of the case cited. A case that has been reversed on appeal, for example, would not be good authority for the point of law for which the decision was reversed. These citation rules are discussed in Appendix A of this book.

The *Bluebook*, however, makes only minimal provision for indicating whether a petition to a higher appellate court for review, such as a writ of certiorari to the United States Supreme Court, was granted or denied. In fact, the *Bluebook* rule is that denials of certiorari or other discretionary appeals should be omitted from a citation, "unless the decision is less than two years old or the denial is particularly relevant."[28] The Texas rules for citation of applications for review to the Supreme Court of Texas or the Texas Court of Criminal Appeals are very different from the basic *Bluebook* rule. The Texas rules are discussed next.

B. Texas Subsequent History Notation

The disposition by the Texas Supreme Court of cases appealed to the court may be important indicators of the weight of authority of an opinion by the intermediate appellate court. A prominent instance where the *Greenbook* imposes different citation rules than the *Blue-*

---

28. *Bluebook*, *supra* note 13, R. 10.7, at 101.

book is the notations for how applications for review are treated when there is no opinion by the Texas Supreme Court on the merits.[29] The practice of including in citations to cases the presence or absence of a writ or petition for review and disposition of any writ or petition dates back to the 1890s.[30]

Until the Texas Rules of Appellate Procedure were revised in 1997, the term used for the application for review on appeal to the Texas Supreme Court was "application for writ of error." The notations used for various treatments of applications for writs of error varied in style and meaning from time to time. For cases from June 14, 1927, until August 31, 1997, the notation "writ ref'd" (writ refused) means the judgment of the court of civil appeals or the court of appeals is correct and has precedential value equal to that of the Texas Supreme Court itself. Review of applications for writs of error was obligatory from September 1, 1892 through June 30, 1917 and from June 14, 1927 through June 19, 1987. Several notations indicating refusal (aside from "writ ref'd") or dismissal were used at various times when review was obligatory. Since obligatory review requires some review on the merits, those notations imply approval of the judgment below and thus have precedential value. Review was made discretionary as of June 20, 1987,[31] with the Texas Supreme Court putting the standard into practice on January 1, 1988. As in other jurisdictions, dispositions denying or dismissing applications for discretionary review have no bearing on the merits of the opinion below.[32] Appendix E to the *Greenbook* supplies the notations, the significance of the notations, and the dates during which the notations were used.[33]

---

29. *Greenbook, supra* note 9, R.4.4., at 22. When the Supreme Court of Texas or the Court of Criminal Appeals granted review and rendered an opinion, the standard *Bluebook* rules apply.

30. James Hambleton, *Notations for Subsequent Histories in Civil Cases*, 65 Tex. B.J. 694, 694 n.2 (2002).

31. Act of June 20, 1987, 70th Leg., R.S., ch. 1106, § 1, 1987 Tex. Gen. Laws 3804, 3804 (effective June 20, 1987 (codified at Tex. Gov't Code Ann. § 22.001 et seq (West 2004)).

32. *Loram Maint. of Way, Inc. v. Ianni*, 210 S.W.3d 593, 596 (Tex. 2006).

33. The history of writs and petitions for review in Texas is very complex and cannot be covered in detail here. A thorough study of the history and

For cases since September 1, 1997, the procedure for application for review on appeal is called a "petition for review." The revised rules specify some notations to be used by the Supreme Court of Texas when a petition for review is refused, denied, or dismissed for want of jurisdiction. The notation "petition refused" means that "the court of appeals' judgment is correct and that the legal principles announced in the opinion are likewise correct." Further, "[t]he court of appeals' opinion in the case has the same precedential value as an opinion of the Supreme Court."[34] The notation "petition denied" means "the Supreme Court is not satisfied that the opinion of the court of appeals has correctly declared the law in all respects, but determines that the petition presents no error that requires reversal or that is of such importance to the jurisprudence of the state as to require correction."[35] However, since denial or dismissal of a petition is discretionary, notations indicating denial or dismissal are not indications of the court's decision on the merits of the opinion of the lower court.[36] A number of other notations are used for cases in which petitions were struck, dismissed, withdrawn, or otherwise disposed of without review on the merits. Other notations indicate whether no petition was filed or the period in which a petition may be filed has not yet passed. See Appendix D of the *Greenbook* for the full list of possible notations, their basis in the rules, and their meaning.

Since 1981, when the Texas courts of civil appeals were given intermediate appellate jurisdiction for criminal appeals and renamed the Texas courts of appeals, notations have also been required for petitions for discretionary review to the Texas Court of Criminal Appeals. These notations have no precedential value. The notations for petitions for discretionary review in the Texas Court of Criminal Appeals are listed in Rule 4.5. of the *Greenbook*.

The researcher in Texas case law must determine the disposition of applications for writ of error or petitions for review and properly

---

the weight of the various notations is provided by Dylan O. Drummond, *Citation Writ Large*, 20 App. Advoc. 89 (2008).

34. Tex. R. App. P. 56.1(c) (West 2003).

35. Tex. R. App. P. 56.1(b)(1) (West 2003).

36. *Loram Maint. of Way, Inc. v. Ianni*, 210 S.W.3d 593, 596 (Tex. 2006).

include them in a citation to a case. This information is found in an annual publication, West's *Texas Subsequent History Table*. For more recent cases, the table is supplemented by cumulative subsequent history tables in the advance sheets to *Texas Cases* and, for very recent cases, in the advance sheets of the *Texas Supreme Court Journal*, the *Slip Opinions of the Courts of Criminal Appeals of Texas*, and the lists of orders in the advance sheets of *Texas Cases*. The notations also may often be obtained online, by using KeyCite in Westlaw or Shepard's in LexisNexis, although the eleventh edition of the *Greenbook* states as a practice tip "it is best to consult West's *Texas Subsequent History Table*."[37]

Appendix A of this book provides full lists of notations for writs and petitions and discusses their use in citations.

---

37. *Greenbook, supra* note 9, at 21, 24.

Chapter 5

Researching Judicial Opinions

I. Introduction

Much legal research requires finding reports of judicial opinions. The skilled researcher may find some cases using one resource and then use others to find additional relevant cases. The method of searching using keyword searches in full-text case databases often yields some useful cases, but often misses cases the researcher needs to find. The tools discussed in this chapter were developed to allow the researcher to search for cases more comprehensively. The legal information for the United States is so well organized and interconnected by these tools that it is often said that one good case is all that is needed to start a process that will find essentially all relevant authority.

II. West Key Numbers and the American Digest System

For over a century, the best developed resource for finding cases has been the West American Digest System. Each digest in the system combines two features to create a powerful finding tool. These features are "headnotes" and "topics and key numbers."

A. Headnotes

Headnotes are abstracts of points of law discussed in a case. The abstracts might be brief passages copied directly from the opinion or they might be brief summaries written by a West editor. The point of law abstracted in a headnote might be the holding of the case, but it might be drawn from discussion of a point of law not essential to the holding or judgment in the case. This is one reason it is essential to read and understand any case relied upon; a case can never be cited based just on a reading of the headnotes.

B. Topics and Key Numbers

The second essential feature of the digest system is the West topic and key number system. This is a subject classification system developed by West to classify all of American law into over 400 broad topics, which are subdivided into narrow classifications identified by key numbers. See Figure 5-1 for part of a page from the *Texas Digest, 2d*. The editor who creates the headnotes for a case assigns topic and key number identifiers to each headnote. Because all cases reported in West National Reporter System reporters have been assigned topics and key numbers since the late nineteenth century, a very powerful case-finding tool has been created in the West Key Number Digest System.

C. West Digest System and the Digests of Other Jurisdictions

The West Key Number Digest System is composed of numerous digests. There is a current digest for each of the states (a few smaller states share a digest with a neighboring state); for several of the West regional reporters; for the federal court system; and for certain specialized courts or topics. There is also a master digest, the *Decennial Digest*, which combines the coverage of all the digests. All digests do the same thing for the jurisdictions they cover. They publish all of the headnotes for opinions reported in West case reporters for their jurisdictions, with each headnote placed together with all other headnotes assigned the same topic and key number. Once the topic and key number for an issue has been found, the headnotes can be read

Figure 5-1. Page from *Texas Digest, 2d*

42B Tex D 2d—177   **PROPERTY**   ☞10

For references to other topics, see Descriptive-Word Index

Tex.Civ.App.–Galveston 1955. Those who were in possession of money at time they were arrested by sheriff, were legally presumed to be the owners of the money.
Cook v. Kern, 277 S.W.2d 946, affirmed 287 S.W.2d 174, 155 Tex. 360.

Possession of personalty is prima facie evidence of title to the personalty, and the possessor of the personalty will recover against the claims of any one who fails to establish a better title to the personalty than the possessor.
Cook v. Kern, 277 S.W.2d 946, affirmed 287 S.W.2d 174, 155 Tex. 360.

Tex.Civ.App.–Galveston 1954. The failure of a party to render land for taxes is a fact admissible on the issue of ownership.
Humble Oil & Refining Co. v. Fantham, 268 S.W.2d 239, dismissed.

☞10. Seisin or possession and incidents thereof.

Library references
C.J.S. Property §§ 27–31, 33.

C.A.5 (Tex.) 1954. Constructive possession of an intangible asset is legal fiction predicated solely upon the owner's right of possession.
Green v. H. E. Butt Foundation, 217 F.2d 553.

Tex.App.–Fort Worth 2004. "Constructive possession" is that which exists without actual personal occupation of land or without actual personal present dominion over a chattel, but with an intent and capability to maintain control and dominion.
Mehan v. WAMCO XXVIII, Ltd., 138

Tex.Civ.App.–Hous. [1 Dist.] 1979. Actual possession to satisfy requirements of prior possession may be through agents or tenants.
Walsh v. Austin, 590 S.W.2d 612, dismissed.

Tex.Civ.App.–Hous. [1 Dist.] 1973. Prior possession may be established through the possession of owner's tenants or agents.
Corder v. Foster, 505 S.W.2d 645, ref. n.r.e.

Tex.Civ.App.–Austin 1980. Possession or the right to possess property may often coexist with legal title but, in a legal sense, the terms are never synonymous.
Crenshaw v. Swenson, 611 S.W.2d 886, ref. n.r.e.

Tex.Civ.App.–Dallas 1975. A person is in possession of a chattel if he has control of it and intent to exercise control and the possessor need not have immediate physical control if someone else is exercising that control in his behalf.
Yarbrough v. John Deere Indus. Equipment Co., 526 S.W.2d 188.

Tex.Civ.App.–Amarillo 1978. In Texas, distinction between seisin in deed and in law is not known; legal title vests owner with seisin and possession which he retains unless divested by actual possession taken and held by another with result that a conveyance by deed gives constructive possession to grantee, who is deemed to be in actual possession even though neither grantee nor anyone under him is actually residing on or occupying land.
Huddleston v. Fergeson, 564 S.W.2d 448.

Source: *West's Texas Digest, 2d.* Reprinted with permission of Thomson Reuters.

to identify cases deserving investigation. The citation to the cases is printed at the end of each headnote.

The first step is determining which digest to use. Researchers looking for cases on state law will choose a digest specifically for that state or, possibly, a digest for the cases reported in the West regional reporter including that state. If searching for Texas cases, choose the *Texas Digest, 2d,* or, for cases before 1935, the *Texas Digest.* There is no digest covering the whole of the *South Western Reporter, 3d* or its predecessors, but for some regional reporters there are digests for all the cases published in the regional reporter. An example is the *South Eastern Digest, 2d,* preceded by the original *South Eastern Digest* for cases prior to 1935. For some other regional reporters there is no second edition digest, but there was a digest that was discontinued at some point. For example, for the *Southern Reporter, 2d*, there is no current digest; the *Southern Digest* can only be used for cases up to its discontinuance in 1988. For cases since that date, the digests for individual states within the region must be used.

If looking for cases only from the federal courts, use West's *Federal Practice Digest, 4th*, which covers all cases reported in West's *Supreme Court Reporter, Federal Reporter, 3d, Federal Supplement, 2d*, and the reporters for specialized federal courts and topics. The *Federal Practice Digest, 4th* is the fifth in a series of digests of federal decisions. The five digests, with slightly differing titles,[1] cover a certain span of years and they are non-cumulative. If cases from years before the coverage of the current digest are needed, the earlier digests must be used. The *Supreme Court Reporter* has its own digest, which may be useful if the researcher is looking only for opinions by the U.S. Supreme Court.[2]

Searching is sometimes best done in a specialized digest, such as West's *Bankruptcy Digest*. The comprehensive coverage of the *Decennial Digest*, a master digest combining the contents of all the digests, is useful when the case law on a certain topic is very thin and the researcher needs to cast as wide a net as possible.

All the digests in the West American Digest System share the same topic and key number classification system. The researcher who has found relevant cases in one jurisdiction can find cases in other jurisdictions by using the digests for those jurisdictions.

---

1. In chronological order, these digests are *Federal Digest, Modern Federal Practice Digest, Federal Practice Digest, 2d, Federal Practice Digest, 3d,* and *Federal Practice Digest, 4th.*

2. An exception to the general use of the West digests is that a researcher seeking only U.S. Supreme Court cases might also use the digest for the *Lawyers' Edition*, which uses its own classification system.

III. Research in the *Texas Digest, 2d*

A researcher uses a topic and key number relevant to an issue to identify cases on that issue in a digest. Often that topic and key number is found in the headnotes of cases already found by other means. Chapter 3 discussed the use of the Notes of Decisions annotations to locate case law interpreting constitutional or code provision. Notes of Decision annotations are used in the same way to find cases interpreting statutes. One or more cases on point may have been found through preliminary reading in secondary authority, through keyword searching in an online database, through conversations with other lawyers, or from other sources. The next stage for the researcher is to use the cases already found to locate more cases on the same point, in the same or in other jurisdictions. The West Key Number Digest System makes this possible.

A. Starting with "One Good Case"

However obtained, "one good case" can open the door to the location of other relevant cases. That one good case will, of course, cite other cases as authority in the opinion; these must be considered. Checking a citator, such as Shepard's or KeyCite (see Chapter 9), will reveal the cases that have cited the case. Most important of all for extending research to locate additional Texas cases is using the *Texas Digest, 2d* or, for cases before 1935, the original *Texas Digest*.[3]

1. Locate the Topic and Key Number in a Digest

Recall that each case in a West reporter has headnotes, each with a topic and key number for the legal issue expressed in the part of the opinion abstracted in the headnote. If a relevant case has been found, the headnotes for that case will be reprinted in the *Texas Digest, 2d*.

---

3. The *Texas Digest* and *Texas Digest, 2d* are non-cumulative, meaning the cases in the *Texas Digest* are not included in the *Texas Digest, 2d*.

Look in the volume containing the topic and key number for a particular headnote to find the headnotes for all other cases in Texas on that topic, up to the cut-off date for publication in the digest volume. Peruse these headnotes to locate the cases from the relevant courts, in chronological order. Finally, use the case citations included in the headnotes to find and read the full printed opinions.

A tip for improving the results from digest searches is to look at the several key numbers on either side of the key number from the original headnote. The key number system is a subject classification system, and the adjacent key numbers will be on closely related topics and may contain additional relevant cases.

The "one good case" need not be a Texas case. It might be a case on the same point from some other state. The digest system allows searching for Texas cases on that issue using the *Texas Digest, 2d.* Alternatively, the Texas researcher who is not satisfied with the Texas cases found might search for cases from other jurisdictions by searching the digests for other jurisdictions.

2. Update the Topic and Key Number Search

Start updating by checking the pocket part of the digest volume for recent cases relevant to your search. The pocket part includes any headnotes added since the publication of the main volume. If a pocket part would be too bulky to fit in the book, a separate cumulative pamphlet will be placed next to the volume supplemented. The next step in updating in print is to check the West reporter advance sheets for the period since the publication of the pocket parts. Each of these will contain a Topic and Key Number table for the headnotes of cases included in the advance sheets. For example, updating Texas cases requires checking the advance sheets to *Texas Cases* or the *South Western Reporter, 3d,* published since the pocket parts in the *Texas Digest, 2d.*

B. Using the Table of Cases Volumes

There will be times when case law research begins in a digest. The issue might be one not covered adequately by secondary authority, relevant statutory law might not have been found, and keyword searches online might have been unsuccessful. Even if one or more of these approaches has yielded useful results, the digests can be used to supplement those results. The finding tools in the digests might suggest useful theories and doctrines developed in lines of cases not found by the other search techniques.

The digests are designed for beginning the search for cases. Each digest comes with several tools for locating relevant cases. The simplest of these is the table of cases, found near the end of each digest set. If the researcher knows the last name of a party in the citation to the case, that name can be looked up in the alphabetically arranged table. Once the case name is found in the table, the entry points to the location of the headnote in the digest. Other finding tools, discussed below, require more thought on the part of the researcher.

C. Using the Descriptive-Word Index

The Descriptive-Word Index allows you to identify relevant topics and key numbers using search terms. The Descriptive-Word Index volumes are located near the end of the *Texas Digest, 2d* set.

1. Develop a List of Search Terms

Recall from Chapter 1 that an early stage in the research process is developing terms to be used in searching in various resources. When developing a list of terms, consider the types of terms that are used in the index to the resource. The Preface to the Descriptive-Word Index states that the index includes factual and legal terms relating to the parties involved, objects or things involved, the places where the facts arose, the defense to the action or issue, and the relief sought. Remember to think of synonyms and broader and narrower terms related to your initial terms. Figure 5-2 shows part of a page from the Descriptive-Word Index.

Figure 5-2. Page of the Descriptive-Word Index

```
56B Tex D 2d–125                                      PROPERTY
                References are to Digest Topics and Key Numbers

PROPERTY—Cont'd                          PROPERTY—Cont'd
                                         STATUTES—Cont'd
OWNERSHIP and incidents thereof, Propty
    ☞ 7                                     Pari materia construction rule, Statut
  See also heading TITLE TO PROPERTY,          ☞ 223.2(25)
    generally.                              Special and local laws, Const Law ☞ 82
PARTITION. See heading PARTITION,           Titles of laws. See subheading TITLES of
    generally.                                 laws, under this heading.
PARTNERSHIP. See heading
    PARTNERSHIP, PROPERTY.                SUBJECTS of property, Propty ☞ 2
PERSONAL property. See heading           SUBMERGED lands. See heading
    PERSONAL PROPERTY, generally.           SUBMERGED LANDS, generally.
POSSESSION and incidents, Propty ☞ 10
PRELIMINARY injunction, Inj ☞ 138.30     TAXATION. See heading PROPERTY
PUBLIC lands. See heading PUBLIC            TAXES, generally.
    LANDS, generally.                     TENURE, Propty ☞ 8
PUBLIC property. See heading PUBLIC
    PROPERTY, generally.                  TITLE to property. See heading TITLE TO
RAILROADS. See heading RAILROADS,          PROPERTY, generally.
    PROPERTY.                             TITLES of laws,
RETURN of property. See heading            Generally, Statut ☞ 115
    RETURN, PROPERTY.                       Amendatory acts, Statut ☞ 115(3)
RIGHTS of action, Propty ☞ 5.5             Repealing acts, Statut ☞ 115(3)
RIPARIAN and littoral rights. See heading
    RIPARIAN AND LITTORAL RIGHTS,        UNITED States. See heading PUBLIC
    generally.                             PROPERTY, UNITED States.
SALE,                                    VALUE. See heading VALUE, generally.
  Personal property. See heading SALES,
    generally.                           VENDORS and purchasers of real estate. See
  Real property,                           heading VENDOR AND PURCHASER,
    Generally. See heading VENDOR AND       generally.
    PURCHASER, generally.                VENUE. See heading VENUE, generally.
```

Source: *West's Texas Digest, 2d.* Reprinted with permission of Thomson Reuters.

2. Search the Descriptive-Word Index

To search in a digest, look up the search terms developed in the preparatory stage of research. As you look up these terms in the index, some may result in immediate success, with the index pointing to the location of relevant topics in the digest. Not uncommonly, the location will not be indicated under the term, but cross-referenced under another term in the index. It is often useful, especially when searches on the prepared terms are unsuccessful, to scan quickly through an index to see if any terms catch your eye. Researchers recognize significant words more easily than they can generate them. The indexers have very likely included terms you had not thought of for the concepts being searched. It sometimes happens that none of the terms the researcher has listed or has thought of while using the index yields any results. In that case, try using other finding tools discussed below.

3. Check the Pocket Parts of the Descriptive-Word Index

As with all other legal research, the results from the search in the main digest volumes must be updated. Be sure to check the pocket part at the back of each volume of the Descriptive-Word Index. The pocket part may include additional terms and will identify any topics and key numbers added as references for a term since the publication of the main volume. Be sure to check the cover of the pocket part to see if the digest you are using has been supplemented with the most current pocket part.

D. Using the West Outline of the Law and Topical Outlines

Searching with terms in the index to the digest does not always locate relevant cases. An alternative finding tool in the digests is the table of contents, typically found at the beginning of the resource. In the West Key Number Digest System, the master outline for the system is known as the "Outline of the Law." The Outline of the Law starts with seven high-level classes into which West divides all American law,[4] and then divides the classes into subclasses, which are then divided into the more than 400 topics of the digest system. This represents the conceptual organization of the West classification system and highlights a useful feature of all tables of contents. Not only are tables of contents useful outlines to what is contained in a resource, they are also representations of the concepts underlying the organi-

---

4. The seven high level classes are Persons, Property, Contracts, Torts, Crimes, Remedies, and Government.

zation of the resource. The user of any book or research resource should not only study the table of contents as a guide to finding content in that resource, but also for what it reveals about the relationships among the topics covered.

A review of the Outline of the Law may indicate several topics possibly relevant to the search. In addition, the first volume containing a topic presents a detailed outline of the key numbers and their subdivisions. This outline should be perused for key numbers with headings possibly relevant to the issue being researched.

The topic and key number system undergoes periodic revision, as old classifications become too narrow for growing areas of the law or as parts of an older topic grow into new topics deserving independent treatment. In some instances, the original names given the topics have become antiquated or offensive to the modern user and a new term is substituted. For example, the topic "Master and Servant" was quite recently replaced with "Labor and Employment." The revisions are sometimes quite significant. When using a volume of a digest, check the pocket part to see if any change in the classification or name of the topic has occurred since the main volume was published. If searching a digest with topics and key numbers obtained from an older research source, the name of a topic might not appear in the current digest, or the headnotes under the old key numbers may not seem relevant. Look at the introductory pages for each topic for information about changes to the system. If there have been changes, a table is included to translate the older topics and key numbers to the current form.

E. Using Words and Phrases

Another finding tool for locating cases in a digest is a set of volumes called "Words and Phrases." Much litigation turns on the meanings of words or phrases, whether they are from the text of statutes or regulations or they have developed special meanings during the formation of judge-made, common law doctrines. Thus, many headnotes from cases will include statements by courts concerning the interpretation given to words or phrases. Locate these headnotes by searching the alphabetically arranged Words and Phrases volumes. The headnotes interpreting the words or phrases from cases reported in the entire West National Reporter System are also included in a master set titled *Words and Phrases.*

IV. Topic Searching Online

West developed a powerful research system over more than a century as the dominant publisher of legal authority in the United States. The linchpin of this system is the West Key Number Digest System. This system has been integrated into the Westlaw online research system. LexisNexis originated the first computerized legal research system, but it did not start out as a legal publisher. LexisNexis has developed its own headnote and classification system in order to compete with Westlaw and give its users the advantages of this kind of research tool. Either of these systems yields much more complete results than is possible using only keyword searching in full-text databases.

A. Searching Online with West Key Numbers

Westlaw allows doing online what can be done in the traditional print digest system. Several options offered by Westlaw are similar to using the index to a digest.

- When you use the search terms developed in the research process to search the full text of a case database, the computer is actually searching a master index of all the words in documents in the database.
- Westlaw also provides databases consisting solely of the headnotes from cases in various jurisdictions. Searching within the headnotes can be an efficient means of reducing the irrelevant hits found by a keyword search.
- Most similar of all to using a print index to locate relevant topics and key numbers is the option of using a natural language search to identify possibly relevant topics and key numbers.

This option is accessed by clicking on "Key Numbers" at the top of the Westlaw home page.

B. Beginning with a Topical Key Number Search in Westlaw

Also found under "Key Numbers" are two approaches to finding topics and key numbers in subject hierarchies. One, called "West Key Number Digest Outline," provides the standard digest system subject hierarchy, with the top level being the more than 400 topics and lower levels accessible by expanding the topics. Drill down through the hierarchy by expanding each level until the ultimate key numbers are reached.

The alternative approach, called "KeySearch," was developed specifically for Westlaw. KeySearch starts with a smaller number of high level legal specialties. Drill down from the top level through successive levels until a specific topic and key number is reached. Once a topic and key number is reached, click through to a search template and select state or federal jurisdictions in which to search for case headnotes with that topic and key number. Additional keywords can be added to the search.

Subsets of the digest system can also be accessed from the search pages for most case databases. A link in the upper right corner to a "Custom Digest" gives access to the topic hierarchy for searching the cases in the jurisdictions in the particular database.

C. Extending a Search Using Key Numbers Online

Using the topics and key numbers of a case already found in order to find other relevant cases in the digest was discussed above. Similarly, if online research has found a case on point, other cases dealing with the same issue can be found by clicking on the key number link from a headnote dealing with the subject. See Figure 5-3 for an illustration of a headnote with key number links. Clicking on a link brings up a template for selecting jurisdictions to be searched for cases

Figure 5-3. Headnotes on Westlaw with Key Number Links

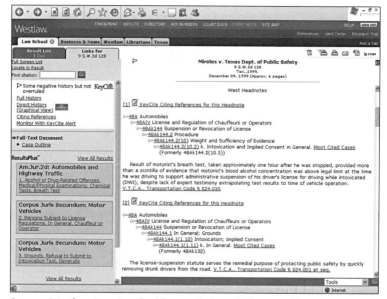

Source: Westlaw. Reprinted with permission of Thomson Reuters.

on the same topic and including additional terms for searching the text of the headnotes.

D. LexisNexis: Using the Topic and Headnote System

LexisNexis has developed a system of headnotes and topics for case searching that somewhat resembles the West digest topic and key number system adapted for use in Westlaw. LexisNexis employs editors to create headnotes for cases. These headnotes are located by any of several methods for finding relevant cases and then examining the headnotes. As in the West topic and key number system, cases on the same narrow topic should all be assigned the same headnote identifiers allowing extension of the search. Some of the connections within the LexisNexis system are generated by computer algorithms. This can result in search results with more irrelevant cases than those in the Westlaw system.

Figure 5-4. Search Tabs in LexisNexis

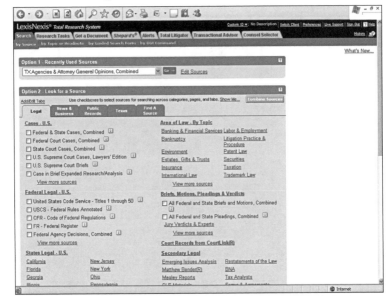

Source: LexisNexis. Copyright 2009 LexisNexis, a division of Reed Elsevier Inc. All Rights Reserved. LexisNexis and the Knowledge Burst logo are registered trademarks of Reed Elsevier Properties Inc. and are used with the permission of LexisNexis.

1. Searching by Topic or Headnote

To search from scratch, select the "Search" tab, then choose either "Topic or Headnote" or "Guided Search Form." See Figure 5-4. If "Topic or Headnote" is chosen, two options are available, "Find a Legal Topic" and "Explore a Legal Topic." "Find a Legal Topic" allows term searching to identify possible topic chains. An example of a topic chain is: All Topics>Criminal Law & Procedure>Search & Seizure>Warrantless Searches>Stop & Frisk>General Overview>. This topic chain serves as the narrow topic identifier for headnotes, similar to the topic and key number assigned to West headnotes. Choosing a topic chain brings up a template where case collections to be searched are selected and additional search terms may be added to further refine the search. The second option, "Explore a Legal Topic," allows drilling down from high level topics to create topic chains at the level used for headnote classification. The same template just mentioned is used to select case collections and to add optional search terms.

2. Using the Guided Search Form

The "Guided Search Form" provides an alternative method of using the headnotes. Select "Cases." At the search screen, check the box "Find points of law only (LexisNexis® Headnotes)," and then enter search terms. A list will appear with cases for which the search terms appear in the text of at least one headnote. After determining which of the cases are relevant and which headnotes deal with your issue, you can then record the topic chain for use in other searches or extend the search.

3. Extending the Search

Extending the search from cases found is similar to the process in Westlaw. If you know the citation to a relevant case, use the tab "Get a Document" to retrieve the case. If you have found cases by searching in a LexisNexis database, searching by "Topic and Headnote," or by using the "Guided Search Form," evaluate the cases for relevance and identify the headnotes relating to your issue. You can then link to other cases identified by LexisNexis editors as relating to the topic by clicking on the "All" icon at the end of the topic chains assigned to the headnote. An alternative is to click on "More like this," which applies a computer algorithm using terms in the headnote. Clicking on "All" or "More like this" will bring you to a template that allows selection of the case collection to be searched and for limitation by date range.

E. Using Citators to Extend Case Research

As a final note, KeyCite and Shepard's are also valuable for finding additional cases dealing with the same issue as a case you have already found. By using a citator, you will find cases that have cited the case. Some of these cases may have dealt with the same issue as the one you are interested in. These can be identified by the notation showing the number of the headnote in your cited case that the citing case addresses. Cases may be found that other methods missed, and the cases may be particularly important in that they are in the same chain of authority and affect the value and meaning of the case citated. See Chapter 9 for discussion of citators.

Chapter 6

Statutory Research

I. Statutes and Codes in American Law

Much law in modern American society is statutory. Statutes, the laws enacted by legislatures, now control many areas once the subject of the common law, and new statutes continue to be passed to address new problems. Statutory law may be either criminal or civil. All laws have consequences for non-compliance. Criminal law violations are prosecuted by the state, while non-compliance with civil laws may give rise to enforcement actions, claims for damages, or other claims by individuals, private organizations, or government agencies. It is important to remember that, although statutory law has replaced the common law for many purposes, the courts have the final authority to decide how a statute is interpreted and whether it complies with constitutional requirements.

A. Session Laws and Codification

As legislatures enact new laws, these statutes are published first as "slip laws." Then they are published in volumes compiling the new laws for the legislative session in chronological order of passage; these compilations are "session laws." Since a chronological collection of public acts covering many decades would be almost impossible to use for research, the State of Texas, like all other states and the federal government, reorganizes the statutes into "codes." Codification involves establishing classifications of the law, determining which parts of the statutes are current law, and placing the current statutes into the proper classifications, with further subdivisions within each broad classification. As new laws are enacted, the code is updated to add new language and to change or remove existing language, as required by the new statutes. Codification allows for effective searching and for maintaining an accessible, current version of the statutory law.

B. Texas Session Laws and Historical Codes

The Texas legislature meets every two years, for no more than 140 days in a regular session. The governor can call additional special sessions, known as "called sessions," of no more than thirty days and limited to consideration of the issues for which they were called. For every session, the enacted laws, called "chapters," are published in volumes of session laws called the *General and Special Laws of the State of Texas*.

The earliest published subject matter classifications of Texas statutes were privately developed. Paschal's *A Digest of the Laws of the State of Texas* was published in several editions between 1866 and 1874 and served as the model for the first official publication. The Legislature of the State of Texas published official "revised statutes" beginning in 1879, with three subsequent revisions by the legislature. An official revision in 1925 resulted in the enactment of the *Revised Texas Statutes of 1925,* comprised of the *Revised Texas Civil Statutes* ("Revised Civil Statutes"), the *Penal Code,* and the *Code of Criminal Procedure.* The *Revised Texas Statutes of 1925* were published in *Vernon's Texas Revised Statutes Annotated.* This *Vernon's* publication, together with numerous subsequent topical revisions and codifications added under a variety of names to the *Vernon's* set, has served as the quasi-official source of Texas statutory law. New laws were placed into *Vernon's Texas Revised Statutes Annotated* as they were enacted. By the 1960s, *Vernon's Texas Revised Statutes Annotated* had become inconsistent and difficult to use, as the legislature sometimes passed new legislation without repealing older parts or making other necessary changes.

C. The Codification Project

In 1963 the legislature ordered a comprehensive project to create subject matter codes to replace the existing *Revised Texas Statutes of 1925*, as updated by *Vernon's Texas Revised Statutes Annotated*. Although the language was to be corrected and updated, the codifiers were directed to transfer the existing statutes to the new codes without changing the substance of the law.[1] This project continues to this day. When it is completed, all the general and permanent statutes will have been organized into twenty-seven subject matter codes. Twenty-six codes have been partially or totally completed and enacted into law, superseding most of the revised statutes as authority.[2] These codes are published as *Vernon's Texas Codes Annotated* (V.T.C.A.), a subset of the comprehensive *Vernon's* black book set. See Table 6-1 for a complete list of the subject matter codes.

It is sometimes necessary to refer to both the new subject codes and the older titles and codes in the course of Texas statutory research. A set of tables near the end of the *Vernon's* set indicates where the various articles of all pre-codification titles and codes have been placed in the current subject codes.

---

1. The reasons for the codification, expressed here in the Texas Agriculture Code, section 1.001(b) are:

"(b) Consistent with the objectives of the statutory revision program, the purpose of this code is to make the agriculture law more accessible and understandable, by:

(1) rearranging the statutes into a more logical order;

(2) employing a format and numbering system designed to facilitate citation of the law and to accommodate future expansion of the law;

(3) eliminating repealed, duplicative, unconstitutional, expired, executed, and other ineffective provisions; and

(4) restating the law in modern American English to the greatest extent possible."

2. *Texas Laws, Past and Present*, Legislative Reference Library of Texas (Jan. 31, 2012), www.lrl.state.tx.us/legis/texasLawTimeline.cfm.

Table 6-1. List of Subject Matter Codes

Enacted, in Full or in Part	Not Yet Enacted
Agriculture Code	Code of Criminal Procedure
Alcoholic Beverage Code	
Business & Commerce Code	
Business Organizations Code	
Civil Practice & Remedies Code	
Education Code	
Election Code	
Estates Code (effective January 1, 2014)	
Family Code	
Finance Code	
Government Code	
Health & Safety Code	
Human Resources Code	
Insurance Code	
Labor Code	
Local Government Code	
Natural Resources Code	
Occupations Code	
Parks & Wildlife Code	
Penal Code	
Property Code	
Special District Local Laws Code	
Tax Code	
Transportation Code	
Utilities Code	
Water Code	

II. Texas Statutory Research

A. The Components of the Current *Vernon's* Set

Most, but not all, of the Revised Civil Statutes, contained in the *Vernon's Texas Revised Civil Statutes Annotated* volumes, have been transferred to the new codes and re-enacted by the legislature. Most of the articles of the former *Vernon's Annotated Penal Code* have been codified into the new *Vernon's Texas Codes Annotated — Penal*, although some articles were codified into other codes. Four "indepen-

Table 6-2. List of Independent Codes

Code of Criminal Procedure

Insurance Code
(partially recodified and repealed by the codification project)

Probate Code
(recodified as Estates Code, Probate Code remains in effect to January 1, 2014)

Business Corporation Act
(partially recodified and repealed by the codification project)

dent codes" have not yet been fully replaced by the new subject matter codes. See Table 6-2 for a list of the independent codes (three of which are contained in one of two series, confusingly called *Vernon's Texas Civil Statutes* and *Vernon's Texas Statutes Annotated*).[3] The researcher must be able to determine whether the current law is to be found in the subject matter codes or in as yet uncodified parts of the Revised Civil Statutes or independent codes. If a statute has been codified in a subject matter code, upon its effective date the section is the official statute and the predecessor in the Revised Civil Statutes, previous *Penal Code*, or an independent code has been repealed. If it has not yet been codified, the article (or section, for the Probate Code) in a title of the Revised Civil Statutes or one of the four independent codes remains the official statute.

B. Research Process Using *Vernon's* in Print

The researcher, especially if a beginning lawyer, might be given an assignment to look up a particular section of a code. That would require finding only the print code volume by reading the book spines for the code title and range of sections in the volumes, turning to the section, and reading the statutory language (and, of course, checking

---

3. The degree to which the codification project has affected the independent codes varies. Refer to the *Greenbook* for details on the status of the independent codes. Note also that *Greenbook* citations to Texas statutes sometimes are different from *Bluebook* form. Texas practitioners must refer to the *Greenbook* for proper citation form.

the pocket parts). Most projects will be more sophisticated and will usually require searching in the *Vernon's* set for statutory authority on an issue and the cases interpreting it.

1. Develop a List of Search Terms

As discussed in Chapter 1, formulate a list of "search terms" based on the facts. Be sure to brainstorm for many search terms, such as by using the journalistic or TARPP approach. As the research project progresses, you will discover new "terms of art" or words or phrases commonly used to describe concepts in the particular topic area.

2. Search the Index

Start in the index volumes, located near the end of the set, using the search terms developed in the earlier stages of the research process. Some of the terms will be found and supply citations to the subject codes, independent codes, or Revised Civil Statutes, while others will give cross-references to another term. Be sure to follow the cross-references.

The index contains a useful feature for locating precise phrases or combinations of terms. That is the Words and Phrases portion of the index, found alphabetically under "Words." If searches in the rest of the index are not successful, the Words and Phrases section should be tried.

The citations found in the index will be to an abbreviation of a code or title, plus a section or article number.[4] A table at the beginning of each index volume gives the full name corresponding to each abbreviation. For example, "H&S 481.308" is the citation for Health and Safety Code, section 481.308.

---

4. Subject codes are organized into sections. The Revised Civil Statutes are organized into articles, which may be further subdivided into sections. The independent codes are organized into articles, except for the Probate Code, which is organized into sections.

3. Find and Read Statutory Text

The sections or articles identified by searching the index are found by locating the volumes with the name of the particular code or title on the spine and looking at the range of section or article numbers contained in each volume. The sections or articles are arranged by number within a volume. Once the relevant statutes have been found, you must read them carefully. Statutory language is compact but often complex. Several readings are usually required to get a good understanding. The language of statutes is necessarily general. Consider how the general language may apply to the specific facts of your research problem.

Before reading a section or article of a statute, scan the definitions section found in most statutes so you will recognize a defined term when you see it. To better understand a section or article in context, read at least the introductory sections of the statute and also the sections on either side of the ones your initial search has led you to. If the statute has a table of contents, scanning that may reveal other sections or articles that you should read. For fairly short statutes, it is wise to read all of the sections or articles to get the overall context and be sure of not missing anything relevant to your issue.

When reading a section or article with a number of elements or factors listed, go immediately to the end of the list and see whether the connector between the last two items is "and" or "or." If the connector is "and," all the elements or factors must be present to satisfy the condition. If the connector is "or," any of the elements or factors will satisfy the condition. Determining this in advance allows you to read with greater comprehension and efficiency.

At the end of every section or article is a legislative summary, citing the original enactment and any subsequent amendments to the language of the statute, along with the effective dates of the enactment and all amendments. This information is necessary for legislative history research, the subject of the next chapter. The citations to amending acts are also needed if the researcher needs to reconstruct the language of a statute as it appeared at some earlier time. For example, if a cause of action arose in 2001 and the section or article was amended by an act in 2003, the researcher would start with the current language and use the text of the 2003 amendment to reconstruct the statute as is read in 2001.

4. Update Statutory Texts Found

Be sure to check the pocket part to the volume to see if the statute has been changed by legislation since the cutoff date of the legislation included in the bound volume. While you are doing this, check the cover of the pocket part to see whether the contents include all the laws of the most recent session of the legislature. If they do not, or if a session is in progress, look on the shelves after the *Vernon's* set for paper bound volumes of *Vernon's Texas Session Law Service*. This service quickly publishes new acts. When a new act amends the text of current statutes, the session law service prints the new wording in italics and prints the language replaced in brackets and with a strike through.

The service also contains news about recent, significant legislation; a listing of acts for the session; a disposition table showing where in the *Vernon's* codes or revised statutes the sections from the chapter will be placed (the text of some new chapters will be broken up, with different sections placed in different places in the codes); a table of sections in the codes affected by legislation during the session; a table of earlier acts of the legislature affected by the new acts of the session; a table showing the bill numbers of all chapters enacted (important for legislative history research); and an index for the session. The session law service pamphlets are cumulative throughout the session, so only the most recent one needs to be used.

5. Find Cases Interpreting Texas Statutory Law

The job of the courts is to say what the law is. Much litigation turns on what the words in a statute mean, whether a certain matter falls under a statute, or whether a statute is unconstitutional or void as against public policy. The researcher must, therefore, examine the cases interpreting the statute. The researcher needs to know how the courts have interpreted its language and applied the statute to particular facts in order to understand what the statute means and predict how a court would decide cases brought under the statute. Fol-

Figure 6-1. *Vernon's* Code Section with Annotations

§ 51.072. Effect of Forfeiture

In cases of forfeiture, the original obligations and penalties are as binding as if no forfeiture occurred.

Acts 1977, 65th Leg., p. 2423, ch. 871, art. I, § 1, eff. Sept. 1, 1977.

Historical and Statutory Notes

Prior Laws:
Acts 1895, p. 63.
G.L. vol. 10, p. 793.
Rev.Civ.St.1895, art. 4218*l*.
Acts 1897, pp. 39, 184.

Rev.Civ.St.1911, art. 5423.
Acts 1919, p. 314.
Acts 1941, 47th Leg., p. 351, ch. 191, § 3.
Acts 1951, 52nd Leg., p. 92, ch. 59, § 2.
Vernon's Ann.Civ.St. art. 5326.

Library References

Public Lands ☞173(21).
WESTLAW Topic No. 317.
C.J.S. Public Lands § 198.

Texts and Treatises
60 Texas Jur 3d, Pub Land § 124.

Notes of Decisions

In general 1

1. In general

In an action to try title to land, the fact that the land commissioner had forfeited the sale to the party under whom plaintiff claimed was not conclusive against him, but he could show that the attempted forfeiture was unauthorized and of no effect. Bumpass v. McLendon (Civ.App. 1907) 45 Tex.Civ.App. 519, 101 S.W. 491.

Forfeiture for nonpayment of interest, as authorized by Vernon's Ann.Civ.St. art. 5326, restored it to public domain, notwithstanding provision for reinstatement of claims on paying the amount due or provisions of Vernon's Civ.St. 1914, art. 5423a, for repurchase by owner, and one who had been granted permit to prospect for oil and gas, on lands so forfeited, was not liable to owner on his subsequent repurchase for amount allowed owner of surface by art. 5904h, after repurchasing without minerals, in view of art. 5920g. Boykin v. Southwest Texas Oil & Gas Co., 1923, 256 S.W. 581.

Source: *Vernon's Statutes and Codes Annotated*. Reprinted with permission of Thomson Reuters.

lowing every statutory section or article in *Vernon's* are annotations, which provide a number of research references to help the researcher understand the meaning of the statute. See Figure 6-1 for a *Vernon's* section and annotations.

The annotations contain "Notes of Decisions." These are the headnotes from West reporters for cases that have dealt with the section or article. The Notes of Decisions are often divided into several classes of issues. Within each class, headnotes are arranged by court of origin, in chronological order for each court. The researcher can quickly scan these for the most relevant cases, concentrating on the courts with mandatory authority and usually focusing on the most recent, relevant cases. The headnotes can also provide a quick overview of the historical development of lines of cases. Each headnote contains a citation to the case. You must read the cases. It is not acceptable to cite to a case based only on the headnotes, a practice that could lead to serious mistakes and even malpractice.

If you are researching a section of a subject code, you will often need to review the cases interpreting the predecessor article or section in the Revised Civil Statutes or independent codes. The Notes of Decisions for the predecessor statutes were not carried over into the annotations for the codified, enacted subject code sections in *Vernon's*. To locate the predecessor, use the Derivation Tables, as described in Section C.3. of this chapter.

C. Other Research Tools in *Vernon's*

1. Other Features of the Annotations

The researcher often needs information in addition to case law in order to interpret a statute. The annotations following a code section or an article also contain a "Historical and Statutory Note," showing its origin in legislation prior to the *Texas Revised Statutes of 1925*, its citation in the *Texas Revised Statutes of 1925*, and any amendments during the period between 1925 and the re-enactment of the statute into the current code. The historical note might contain additional information about the enacting legislation or subsequent amendments.

The annotations might also contain a section of "Cross References" to other statutes dealing with similar subjects. Next come "Library References" to the West Digest System topic and key number relating to the subject of the section. "Library References" cite C.J.S. encyclopedia sections, A.L.R. annotations, and other readings in secondary sources. There may also be "Administrative Code References" to *Texas Administrative Code* sections promulgated pursuant to the statute's authority (see Chapter 8 on Administrative Law), citations to law review articles, and other useful information.

2. Popular Name Table

Another very useful finding tool is the Popular Name Table, located at the end of the last index volume. Often, an act is given a statutory short title, by which the act is meant to be called, in addition to the much longer technical title. Also, many well known statutes come to be known by popular names, such as the "Blue Sky Law," a name used for the securities law in many states, or by a descriptive term, such as the "Clean Air Act." Since researchers often come to an index with only these identifiers for an act, the index lists them in the Popular Name Table. The index to *Vernon's* also includes a Legislative Highlights Index, an index to significant legislation in the most recent session of the legislature.

3. Derivation and Disposition Tables

Now that the codification project is almost complete, most cites found in the index will be to a section of a subject code in *Vernon's Texas Codes Annotated*. Some statutes have not yet been codified from *Vernon's Texas Revised Civil Statutes* or the four independent codes mentioned in Section II.A. In those instances, the cites will be to those resources. Sometimes the researcher will need to find the location of a code section's predecessor, perhaps to see exactly how it was worded before codification,[5] or to review the earlier annotations. Many volumes of *Vernon's Texas Codes Annotated* have a derivation table, which shows for each code section the citation for its predecessor in the Revised Civil Statutes or earlier penal or independent codes. In those volumes without derivation tables, the "prior law" annotation for each section indicates the Revised Civil Statutes article or other statute from which the current section is derived. Conversely, the researcher might have a cite for an article of the Revised Civil Statutes or earlier penal or independent codes, perhaps from reading an older case or secondary resource, and need to find its successor in the current subject codes. A Master Disposition Table volume at the end of the *Vernon's* set traces the disposition of each article in the Revised Civil Statutes, earlier *Penal Code,* and the independent codes to its successor in the current subject codes. Disposition tables also appear near the beginning of every volume of *Vernon's Texas Codes Annotated* to show the disposition of former articles to code sections within that volume.

---

5. Some language is changed in the course of codification, although this rewording is not supposed to change the meaning of the statute.

D. Texas Statutes Online

1. State Website

The current version of the Texas statutes is available through a link from the webpage of the Texas legislature.[6] Following the links down to the section level will lead to the text of the statute. There are also zipped files of each code available for download. The FAQ page at the site contains the warning: "The Texas Legislative Council makes no warranty as to the accuracy of the data, and users rely on the data entirely at their own risk."[7] This will surprise many users, but such disclaimers are common on government websites. The researcher would not cite to the text found here as authoritative, but would cite to the text as found in the *Vernon's* set, which functions as a quasi-official publication of the State of Texas. The page also contains a link to an index to the *Sections Affected* database. This database allows checking which existing sections were affected by legislation in recent sessions of the legislature.

2. Texas Statutes on Westlaw

Westlaw contains the *Vernon's* annotated codes and statutes (TX-ST-ANN) as well as unannotated codes and statutes. The statutes repealed before 1987 by the codification project are not available on Westlaw. Refer to the print *Vernon's* if your code research requires finding and studying statutes repealed before 1987 or their annotations. The unannotated database is sometimes convenient, especially when sections with extensive annotations are loading slowly or when you want to print only the statutory text. Most of the time, however, use the annotated version for the features discussed earlier in this chapter. In addition to keyword searching, an expandable table of contents and index are available. The table of contents and the index are often more dependable tools for searching in statutes and should be used in the same manner as the print statutes.

Since the database is complex, reflecting the complexity of the *Vernon's* set itself, the researcher should review the "scope note," accessed

---

6. The address to that website is www.capitol.state.tx.us.
7. The address is www.statutes.legis.state.tx.us/FAQ.aspx.

by clicking on the button with an "i" on it, and read about the contents, effective dates, and tips for searching. The legislative service is available during the biannual sessions of the legislature. As a general rule, online *Vernon's* statutory text and the annotations will be more current than those found in the print volumes and pocket parts. Be sure to check the statement of currentness at the top of any section viewed online.

3. Texas Statutes on LexisNexis

LexisNexis also contains annotated and unannotated versions of the Texas statutes. The annotated version, however, is much less developed than that of Westlaw, with fewer case abstracts (LexisNexis "case notes") and fewer research references, historical notes, and cross-references than found in *Vernon's*. The statutes repealed before 1991 by the codification project are not available on LexisNexis. Refer to the print *Vernon's* if your code research requires finding and studying statutes before 1991 or their annotations. Like Westlaw, LexisNexis provides access through an expandable table of contents. LexisNexis does not provide an index, however. Although the LexisNexis Texas Statutes & Codes Annotated is a less developed research tool than is Westlaw's *Vernon's* online, it does provide useful references and links to Texas secondary source materials published by LexisNexis.

III. Applying and Interpreting Texas Statutes

A. General Principles of Statutory Construction

As discussed above, statutory research involves finding and reading the text of a statute, finding and analyzing the case law that has applied the statute, formulating the rule of the jurisdiction from this analysis, and applying the rule to the facts. Much litigation turns on the meaning to be given to statutory language. The language may be ambiguous on its face, or its application to a particular fact situation might not be evident. The lawyer in the role of advocate often attempts to inform and persuade the court as to the meaning of the statute as it bears on the client's position.

The courts look to various types of intrinsic and extrinsic evidence in interpreting a statute. Intrinsic evidence is that drawn from the text of the entire statute and its relations to the larger statutory context. Extrinsic evidence is evidence from outside the text that indicates what the legislature intended by the language of the statute. The most cited Texas Supreme Court case on the construction of statutes states:

> We must construe statutes as written and, if possible, ascertain legislative intent from the statute's language. Even when a statute is not ambiguous on its face, we can consider other factors to determine the Legislature's intent, including: the object sought to be obtained; the circumstances of the statute's enactment; the legislative history; the common law or former statutory provisions, including laws on the same or similar subjects; the consequences of a particular construction; administrative construction of the statute; and the title, preamble, and emergency provision.
>
> Additionally, we must always consider the statute as a whole rather than its isolated provisions. We should not give one provision a meaning out of harmony or inconsistent with other provisions, although it might be susceptible to such a construction standing alone. We must presume that the Legislature intends an entire statute to be effective and that a just and reasonable result is intended.[8]

A court will attempt first to give the statute its plain meaning, but can look to other factors. Intrinsic factors mentioned by the court are interpreting the statute as a whole, with the language of the provision interpreted to be consistent with the rest of the statute and consideration of the title, preamble, and emergency provisions of the statute.

---

8. *Helena Chemical Co. v. Wilkins*, 47 S.W.3d 486, 493 (Tex. 2001) (citations omitted).

Among the extrinsic factors mentioned, one frequently used is legislative history—the records of the deliberations of the legislature leading to the enactment. Legislative history research is discussed in detail in Chapter 7.

Courts will also look to various court-developed maxims, known as "canons of construction," in attempting to determine the meaning of language in a statute. These maxims are, however, often contradictory, allowing for choice among rules and uncertainty as to result. The researcher should look to the case law of the jurisdiction to determine how the courts apply canons of construction. A longstanding authority on statutory construction is *Statutes and Statutory Construction*, commonly know as "Sutherland," after its original author.[9]

B. Texas Code Construction Act and Construction of Laws Statute

The Texas statutes provide guides to statutory construction. The codification project, while directed by the legislature to "not alter the sense, meaning, or effect of the statute"[10] in transferring language from the Revised Civil Statutes or penal or independent codes to the new subject codes, also involved rewriting of many statutes for greater clarity. The Code Construction Act[11] provides rules to aid in the construction of the meaning of code sections resulting from the statutory codification project. These rules function much like the traditional canons, as aids to interpretation but not exclusive authority.[12] The Construction of Laws statute[13] provides rules of construction for civil statutes (those Revised Civil Statutes remaining in effect). The Texas researcher will study the cases applying the rules

---

9. The authors of the 7th edition are Norman J. Singer and J.D. Shambie Singer.
10. Tex. Gov't Code Ann. § 323.007(b) (West 2005).
11. Tex. Gov't Code Ann. § 311.001–.034 (West 2005).
12. Tex. Gov't Code Ann. § 311.003 (West 2005).
13. Tex. Gov't Code Ann. § 312.001–.016 (West 2005).

of the Code Construction Act or the Construction of Laws statute to determine the weight and interpretation given to them by the courts of Texas.

IV. Researching Statutes of Other States

The process of researching statutory law is very similar in other states. Some states have both officially published codes and commercial publications. The commercially published codes most useful for research are annotated codes, with features much like those found in *Vernon's*.[14] Officially published codes are often unannotated, but in a few states, such as Montana, the state-published annotated code is the only annotated code available. States differ in how they organize their codes. They might identify all sections only by number, (e.g., Wash. Rev. Code. § 2.08.180), or they might, as in Texas, divide the codified statutes into a number of named codes. Each state also publishes official series of session laws, although the titles given the session laws vary greatly. The researcher must determine which sources are considered official for purposes of citation and to which sources citation is preferred.

State codes are published online by almost all states. Be sure to determine whether these are considered official for purposes of citation and whether these are considered authoritative for purposes of legal research; many states place disclaimers on their online codes stating they should not be relied upon for legal research purposes. Be sure also to check the currency of the online code. State codes are available on Westlaw and LexisNexis, with each typically including an unannotated and an annotated version. If West or LexisNexis publishes an annotated code in print, expect to find that publication on their online services. As in Texas, the online service that does not have

---

14. Few state codes are as complex as the *Vernon's* set. The codification project has greatly complicated the contents and use of *Vernon's*.

access to the annotated code published by its parent company may have a less thoroughly annotated state code online.

V. Researching Federal Statutes

Federal statutes enacted during a session of the United States Congress are known as "public laws." Each public law is cited by the session of the Congress and its number in the chronological order of enactment. Thus, the 670th public law of the 80th Congressional session is Pub. L. No. 80–670. These session laws are published in the *United States Statutes at Large,* cited by volume, page number, and year. The public law just cited is printed at 80 Stat. 931 (1966). It is sometimes necessary to refer to the *United States Statutes at Large* in order to read the original text of a public law before amendments were made by later legislation, to see the language in a public law that amends an earlier public law, or to find statutes that are no longer in effect.

Statutory law of the federal government is codified in the *United States Code* (U.S.C.). The U.S.C. is organized by subject into fifty-one "titles," each title containing a number of sections. Cites to federal statutes include title, section, and year, such as 11 U.S.C. § 541 (2006). The U.S.C. is the official publication and should be cited to, if a law is contained in it, but it is revised fully only every six years, with supplemental volumes published annually.

Because the U.S.C. is published slowly and contains few aids to research, most research is performed in the commercially published *United States Code Annotated* (U.S.C.A.), a West publication, or the *United States Code Service* (U.S.C.S.), a LexisNexis publication. These are annotated codes, enhanced by many aids to research (see discussion of use of annotations in this chapter and in Chapter 3). Although similar, each of these publications has some advantages over the other: the U.S.C.A. case annotations are more comprehensive, while the U.S.C.S. claims to be more selective; the U.S.C.S. references more administrative agency decisions; the U.S.C.S. set contains some non-U.S.C. materials not found in the U.S.C.A.; and other differences. Further, each set primarily refers the researcher to secondary resources published by the publisher. For many purposes, however, the sets are comparable and either may be used.

The finding tools in the U.S.C.A. and U.S.C.S. are the same as those found in the *Vernon's* set and discussed earlier in this chapter; the index, table of contents, and Popular Name Table. Each is updated annually by pocket parts. The U.S.C.A. is included in Westlaw, while the U.S.C.S. is included in LexisNexis. The online version is more current than the print annotated codes. Many researchers find the printed codes more effective for performing statutory research, but a final check should be done online to assure the most current text of the statutes and recently added annotations have been found. The topic of researching current legislation to identify possible changes to the existing code is covered in the next chapter.

VI. Court Rules

Court rules govern all stages of litigation, from filing an action through the completion of appeals. They may dictate everything from the size of the margins in briefs to how a case is submitted to the jury. They are authoritative and must be complied with. A case might be dismissed because of the attorney's failure to comply with the court rules.

A. State and Local Rules

Except for the Texas Code of Criminal Procedure, Texas state court rules are promulgated by the Supreme Court of Texas and the Texas Court of Criminal Appeals. The rules of general application are Texas Rules of Civil Procedure, Texas Code of Criminal Procedure, Texas Rules of Appellate Procedure, and Texas Rules of Evidence. These are found in *Vernon's*, with annotations like those in the codes, as well as in a number of specialized publications. Books of court rules for easy reference by practitioners are often called "deskbooks."

In addition to the rules of general application, local courts may promulgate their own local rules, as long as they are not inconsistent with the state court rules. Local court rules can generally be found at the court's website, in publications compiling the local rules of various courts (e.g., *Texas Rules of Court – Local*), and can be obtained from the clerk of the court. Updates to court rules appear in the advance sheets to *Texas Cases* and *South Western Reporter, 3d,* in the *Texas Bar Journal,* and other sources of legal news. The website of a court should list the most current rules.

The researcher familiar with federal court rules will notice that many state court rules are quite similar to federal rules. Many states have modeled their rules to some extent on the federal rules. The researcher should not assume from this similarity that authority interpreting the application of federal rules can be used for the interpretation of state rules. The researcher must seek relevant authority within the state to interpret the meaning of the state rules. Court rules are written in the same outline form as statutes, are interpreted by judicial decisions, and are the subject of secondary commentary, including the comments of the drafters. Thus, the research process of locating, reading, and interpreting court rules is essentially the same as that used in statutory research.

B. Federal Court Rules

The federal court rules of general application are the Federal Rules of Civil Procedure, Federal Rules of Criminal Procedure, Federal Rules of Bankruptcy Procedure, and Federal Rules of Evidence. These are included in the U.S.C.A. and U.S.C.S. As with the statutory sections in those sets, the annotations provide headnotes of cases interpreting the rules, historical information, and references to secondary sources.

The individual federal courts, including the U.S. Supreme Court, have local rules with which the practitioner before the court must be familiar. These are available at the court webpages, in a number of specialized publications, and from the clerk's office for the court. Court rules are revised from time to time. As with all legal authority, it is essential to determine that the source used is current.

Chapter 7

Bill Tracking and Legislative History

I. Introduction

This chapter begins with an overview of the process by which the Legislature of the State of Texas enacts new laws. Since lawyers identify bills that might affect their client's interests and track the bills as they move through the legislative process, the methods of bill tracking are introduced next. The remainder of the chapter is devoted to research in legislative history. Courts sometimes consider the legislative history of statutes when interpreting statutory language. Legislative history consists of the documents produced during the progress of a bill from introduction to enactment.

II. The Texas Legislative Process

The legislature consists of the Texas Senate, with thirty-one members, and the Texas House of Representatives, with one hundred fifty members. The legislature meets in odd-numbered years. Regular sessions may be no more than 140 days. Special sessions, known as "called sessions," may be called by the governor for periods not to exceed thirty days. During called sessions, the legislature can only consider the matters identified by the governor in the proclamation calling the session.

The procedures for enacting laws in Texas are similar to those of other states and of the United States Congress. Table 7-1 shows the

Table 7-1. How a Bill Becomes Law

Legislative Action	Documents Produced
An idea for a bill is proposed by an arm of the government, a legislator, a group, or an individual. A legislator agrees to sponsor it. The bill is drafted by the legislator, staff attorneys, the Texas Legislative Council, or others.	An introduced **bill** may affect a client's interests. If the language of the bill is changed before enactment, the changes may reveal the intent of the legislature.
The bill is introduced in the House or Senate, numbered, read on the floor of the chamber for the first time, and referred to a committee.	
The committee holds public hearings and studies the bill. The bill may be amended or another draft may be substituted for the original. The committee holds a formal hearing and vote, resulting in a favorable report or unfavorable report.	**Hearings** are recorded on audiotape. **Minutes** of committee meetings are kept. A **bill analysis** is prepared by the bill author or by the research staff of the House Research Organization or the Senate Research Center for any bill reported favorably. The bill analysis contains explanations of current law, the need for legislation, and the effect of the bill. A **fiscal note**, analyzing the fiscal impact of the bill, must be prepared by the Legislative Budget Board for most bills requiring use of state funds or statewide use of local funds. A **committee report**, containing the committee's recommendation and the record of the committee's vote is prepared by the committee.
A bill with a favorable report is scheduled for a second reading and debate on the floor of the House or Senate. The bill may be amended by majority vote of representatives or senators. The bill passes to the third reading.	**A Daily Floor Report** is prepared by the House Research Organization on selected bills scheduled for debate and vote in the House. House and Senate **debates** are recorded on **audiotape**. Some debates are recorded on **video**.
The bill is read for the third time and debated on the floor of the House or Senate. The bill may be amended by two thirds vote of representatives or senators. An approved, amended bill is sent as an "engrossed bill" to the other chamber.	The **House Journal** or **Senate Journal** records the actions on the floor and the votes. The **engrossed bill** is sent to the second chamber.
Essentially the same process is followed in the other chamber, with some procedural differences. The bill may be amended further. If approved by vote of the other chamber, the bill is sent back to the originating chamber.	Documents produced at each stage are the same as those shown above (except the Senate does not have a Daily Floor Report). An **amended bill** is sent to the originating chamber.
A bill with no amendments added in second chamber is sent as an "enrolled bill" to the governor.	
If the bill was amended in the second chamber and the originating chamber accepts all amendments, the bill is enrolled and sent to the governor.	The **enrolled bill** is sent to the governor.

Table 7-1. How a Bill Becomes Law, *continued*

Legislative Action	Documents Produced
If amendments are not accepted, a conference committee is appointed to negotiate matters in disagreement. If the committee agrees on terms, a unified bill includes amendments by the conference committee. A conference committee report is filed and adopted by each chamber.	A **unified bill**, showing markups, is prepared. A **conference committee report**, containing the committee's recommendation of the unified bill, is prepared by the conference committee.
The unified bill is enrolled and sent to the governor.	The **enrolled bill** is sent to the governor.
The governor has ten days (not including Sundays) to act on the bill. If the governor signs the bill, it becomes law. If the governor does not sign within ten days, the bill becomes law automatically.	The governor may produce a **signing statement** or **veto statement**.
If the bill is vetoed by the governor, that veto may be overridden by a two thirds vote of the house and senate.	The **debate** and **vote** are recorded as are other debates and votes.
The enacted bill is assigned a session law number. In Texas, this is called a chapter number. The chapter number is a chronological number showing when the bill was passed in that session of the legislature.	The **session law** is published as a chapter in the General and Special Laws of the State of Texas. The session law is **codified** in a **subject matter code** with other statutes on same topic. Revised Civil Statutes remaining in effect may also be changed by a session law.

steps of the legislative process from the idea for a bill to its enactment into law and the documents produced at each step of the process.

The Texas Legislative Council provides excellent information about the Texas legislative process and access to documents through the *Guide to Texas Legislative Information*.[1] The House Research Organization has published online[2] a very detailed procedural guide to each step of the process. Extensive resources for bill tracking and conducting online legislative history research are available at www.capitol.state.tx.us. The Legislative Research Library of Texas website also contains useful histories, documents, explanatory material, and data.

---

1. This resource is available at www.tlc.state.tx.us/gtli/home.html.

2. House Research Organization, *Focus Report: How a Bill Becomes Law: 80th Legislature* (Feb. 1, 2007), www.hro.house.state.tx.us/focus/hwbill80.pdf.

Table 7-2. Outline for Texas Bill Tracking

---

1. Go the Texas Legislature Online (TLO) website at
   www.legis.state.tx.us/Home.aspx
2. When you know the bill number, do each of the following:
   a. Click on "Bill Lookup."
   b. Select the current legislative session.
   c. Select the type of information desired.
   d. Enter the bill number and submit.
3. When you do not know the bill number, use one of the following approaches:
   a. Click on "Sections Affected," select the current legislative session, select the desired code name or the Revised Civil Statutes option, enter the section or article number, and submit.
   b. Click on "Bill Search," select the current legislative session, and search by subject, author, committee, sponsor, or action.
   c. Click on "Text Search," select the current legislature, check boxes for bill types, formulate topic search terms, and either search by simple keyword search options or use a customized Boolean search.
4. Special features: The TLO page allows you to create lists of bills to be followed, save your searches, and set customized RSS feeds and alerts to your email, cell phone, or PDA.

III. Bill Tracking

A. Bill Tracking in the Texas Legislature

Existing statutory law is subject to change as new laws replacing, amending, or deleting existing laws are passed by the legislature. Attorneys must know how bills introduced in the legislature might affect existing law. Table 7-2 outlines the steps for identifying a pending bill and tracking its progress through the legislature.[3]

---

3. The Texas Legislature Online (TLO) website contains historical bill information, as well as guides to bill tracking and tools for automatic updating of bill status. TLO is available at www.capitol.state.tx.us.

1. Researching with a Bill Number

If you already know the bill number, you can determine its status easily and at no cost at the Texas Legislature Online (TLO) website at www.legis.state.tx.us/Home.aspx. This page has many useful links to information about the House and Senate, search engines for legislative information, and guides to performing bill tracking and legislative history research. Take the time to familiarize yourself with the resources available there.

To get bill tracking information for the bill you are interested in, click on "Bill Lookup." Select the current legislative session and the type of information you want, and enter the bill number. The text of the bill can be selected from the "Information Type" menu. Selecting "History" will produce a full listing of all actions since the introduction of the bill, as well as background information about the bill, such as author, sponsor, subject, committees referred to, outcome of any votes, and date of last action. Selecting "Index to Sections Affected" will provide a list of all current sections of codes and Revised Civil Statutes potentially affected by the bill.

The search page for Bill Lookup also provides phone numbers for the Bill Status Hotline. The hotline is a service the Legislative Research Library of Texas offers while the legislature is in session. Researchers may call the hotline to inquire about the status of pending bills without using the online tools.

2. Searching for and Tracking Pending Bills

The researcher often will not have a bill number, but will need to search for bills that affect existing law. The most useful resource for this purpose is again the Texas Legislature Online (TLO) website at www.legis.state.tx.us/Home.aspx. Several search options are available at the TLO site. See Figure 7-1.

To determine whether any pending legislation could affect a particular part of existing Texas statutory or constitutional law, click on "Sections Affected." This links to a template where specifications are entered in text boxes and drop-down menus. Select the current leg-

Figure 7-1. Texas Legislature Online

Source: Texas Legislature Online website, www.capitol.state.tx.us.

islative session; select the particular code, the constitution, revised statutes, or session laws from the drop-down menu; enter the section or article concerned; and submit.

Two other options are available to find out more generally whether pending legislation will affect an area of the law. The options are "Bill Search" and "Text Search." The "Bill Search" link opens a template in which a subject search can be entered. To enter a subject search, click on "Select subject criteria," which will open a new window. Select a category of subject types to be searched. A list of classifications will appear. Select one or more desired classifications and click on "OK." This enters the classifications in the main search template. Select either "and" or "or" to determine whether the search must identify bills satisfying both criteria or only one of the two, then click on "Search." If any bills meet the criteria, a list appears with a short description. Clicking on the hyperlinked bill number opens the full bill history record.

Bills on a topic of interest can also be searched by using the "Text Search" option. As with any full-text search, formulate search terms before beginning. At the TLO page, click on "Text Search" to get to the search template. In the template, select the current legislature, check boxes for bill types desired, and enter the search terms, either using one of several simple keyword search options or by formulating a customized Boolean search query. The Boolean search conventions differ considerably from those used in Westlaw or LexisNexis, so be sure to click on the help feature, indicated by a "?" link, for detailed information about proper use of the Boolean option.

Once bills of interest have been identified in the current legislature, they can be tracked throughout the session. One method is simply to return to the page from time to time and use "Bill Lookup" to check on status, but the legislature provides more sophisticated tracking tools through the TLO page. The researcher can create lists of bills to be followed, save searches, and set customized RSS feeds and bill action and meeting alerts to email, cell phone, or PDA.

The traditional print tool for identifying and tracking new legislation is *Vernon's Texas Legislative Service*. Its usefulness has been largely superseded by the powerful online tools provided by the legislature, but it can still be convenient as a first step in identifying pending legislation and the critical bill number for the researcher who is working with the *Vernon's* set in print, as many experienced researchers prefer to do. *Vernon's Texas Legislative Service* is available on Westlaw in more current form than the print publication for bill tracking during legislative sessions. The legislative service and other current and archival bill tracking databases are found by following the directory trail: Directory>U.S. State Materials>Texas>Statutes & Legislative Materials. LexisNexis also provides Texas bill tracking databases. Bill text and bill tracking databases are available on the "Texas" tab, under the link "Find Statutes, Regulations, Administrative Materials & Court Rules."

B. Bill Tracking in the U.S. Congress

The U.S. Congress makes excellent tools available for searching bills, obtaining the texts of various versions of bills, and tracking bill status. The Thomas website, at http://thomas.loc.gov, is maintained by the Library of Congress. Thomas allows full-text searching and searching by bill number, standard subject term, words or phrases, sponsor, committee, date of introduction, and stage in the legislative process. Be sure to read the searching instructions before beginning. The FDsys website, at www.gpo.gov/fdsys, is the official website of the United States Government Printing Office. FDsys provides published versions of bills introduced in the current and previous sessions of Congress, as well as histories of bill actions reported in the *Congressional Record*.

Westlaw provides many federal bill text and bill tracking databases. These are most easily found by following the trail: Directory>U.S. Federal Materials>Bill Tracking. LexisNexis also provides federal bill tracking databases. These are most easily found by starting at the "Search" tab, opening the "By Source" tab, clicking on "Federal Legal —U.S.," and clicking on "Legislative Histories and Materials."

A traditional print tool for bill tracking and for historical information about bills is the *Congressional Index*, published by C.C.H. The *Congressional Index* is available in most law libraries.

IV. Texas Legislative History Research

Much litigation turns on the meaning of statutes. When the meaning of words or phrases is not clear, the courts will look to other statutes in the jurisdiction and for court opinions that have already interpreted the statute. If these authorities do not resolve the issue, courts may look to other evidence as aids to interpretation. One type of evidence a court may consider is legislative history, the documentary record of the passage of a bill through the legislative process, as evidence of the intent of the legislature.

Courts differ in the extent to which they will consider the documents produced during the legislative process as evidence of legislative intent. In Texas, statutory law on construction of statutes explicitly permits the courts to consider legislative intent and legislative history. The Code Construction Act states "a court may consider among other matters" legislative history in construing the substantive codes.[4] The Construction of Laws statute provides that in construing civil statutes (that is, the Texas Revised Civil Statutes remaining in effect), "a court shall diligently attempt to ascertain legislative intent."[5] Many Texas court opinions thus look to legislative history as one aid in interpreting statutes.

Legislative history research uses many of the tools already discussed for bill tracking. Rather than following a bill through the current legislature, the researcher in legislative history must start with information from current statutory resources to discover the bill or bills that became the statute in question. Once the bill number and legislative session are known, the timeline of legislative actions can be determined and available documents obtained and studied.

The availability of legislative history sources in Texas varies greatly, depending on the years in which the legislation was enacted. The record prior to 1973 is very sparse, while information from recent legislatures is readily available online. The following pages discuss the sources of legislative history, followed by a description of the research process.

A. Sources of Texas Legislative History

The documents produced during the legislative process were identified in Table 7-1. These documents, their significance, and where they may be found are now discussed in more detail. Since much of the work done by the legislature is done by committees, many of the documents are produced for or by committees as they consider and recommend bills. The *Guide to Texas Legislative Information* (G.T.L.I.) website provides access information for legislative documents, publications, and recordings at www.tlc.state.tx.us/gtli/home.html.

---

4. Tex. Gov't Code Ann. § 311.023(3) (West 2005).
5. Tex. Gov't Code Ann. § 312.005 (West 2005).

1. Versions of Bills

The changes made to a bill as it passes through the legislative process can yield insights to the intent of the legislature. The "introduced version" should be obtained for comparison with later versions.

All bills must be considered by a committee. The committee may recommend amendments to the bill in the committee's report to the chamber. Bills reported with a favorable recommendation are scheduled for floor debate and vote. Additional amendments may be proposed and voted on during the debate on the floor. If the chamber votes to approve the bill and amendments, the amended bill is sent as an "engrossed version" to the other chamber.

The second chamber follows a similar process of committee consideration and report, floor debate, and vote. Amendments may be made to the bill during consideration in the second chamber. The engrossed version resulting from passage through the second chamber is sent back to the originating chamber, which may either accept the bill, as amended, or reject the amendments. If the originating chamber accepts the engrossed bill from the second chamber, that version becomes the "enrolled version" and is sent to the governor for signing. If the originating chamber does not accept the changes, a "conference committee," consisting of members of both houses, is formed to attempt to reconcile the differences.

If the conference committee agrees on a unified version, that becomes the enrolled version sent to the governor. Figure 7-2 shows the caption and part of the text of an introduced bill. Note these features: the bill number, H.B. No. 2766; the name of the bill author, (Representative) Eiland; the mandatory caption, "A Bill to be Entitled an Act"; and the enacting clause, "Be it Enacted by the Legislature of the State of Texas," without which no bill can be enacted into law.

2. Committee Hearings

All official committee actions and votes must be open to the public. Committees often solicit testimony for public hearings. Since 1973, testimony at hearings has been recorded on audio tapes. The

Figure 7-2. Introduced Bill

80R7925 KLA-D

By: Eiland   H.B. No. 2766

A BILL TO BE ENTITLED

AN ACT

relating to the location at which certain courts may conduct proceedings following certain disasters.

BE IT ENACTED BY THE LEGISLATURE OF THE STATE OF TEXAS:

SECTION 1. Subchapter A, Chapter 24, Government Code, is amended by adding Section 24.033 to read as follows:

Sec. 24.033. LOCATION OF PROCEEDINGS FOLLOWING CERTAIN DISASTERS. (a) In this section, "first tier coastal county" and "second tier coastal county" have the meanings assigned by Section 2210.003, Insurance Code.

---

tapes are available from the house or senate media offices. Written transcripts are generally not available. Some committee hearings have been webcast and recorded as video since 2001. Archives are available at committee websites.

Committees typically prepare minutes of their meetings. The minutes are quite summary, but do indicate what matters were considered by a committee at a meeting. Committee minutes, witness lists, and hearing notices are available online at the TLO website, beginning with the 75th legislature. The Legislative Reference Library of Texas has minutes for senate committees from 1973 and the Office of the House Committee Coordinator has house committee minutes, some going back as far as 1960.

3. Bill Analyses

All bills, with the exception of house appropriation bills, that are reported favorably by a committee must be accompanied by a "bill analysis." Bill analyses are commonly prepared by the author or by research staff of the House Research Organization or the Senate Research Center. A bill analysis summarizes the background of current law and facts giving rise to the need for legislation and how the bill addresses the problem, explains the content and policies of the bill, contains a statement of rule-making authority to be granted to administrative agencies or commissions by the bill, and summarizes the amendments proposed by the committee. Bill analyses are included when committees issue their reports on bills to the chamber. Bill analyses may also be produced when bills are introduced. Figure 7-3 is an example of a bill analysis.

4. Fiscal Notes

Fiscal notes, analyzing the fiscal impacts of the proposed legislation, are required for any bill, with the exception of general appropriations bills, that would require use of state funds or have a statewide effect on local government funds. Fiscal notes are prepared by the Legislative Budget Board at the request of committee chairs. Fiscal notes are included when committees issue their reports on bills to the chamber. Several fiscal notes may be produced during the legislative process, as the bill is introduced and as it is considered by committees and engrossed with floor amendments. Figure 7-4 is an example of a fiscal note.

5. Committee Reports

In addition to the bill analysis, fiscal note, other evidentiary material, and text of the bill with any amendments, bills approved by a committee are sent to the chamber with a printed committee report. The committee report contains the committee's recommendation and record of votes.

6. Daily Floor Reports

During the legislative session, the House Research Organization prepares a daily floor report summarizing and analyzing selected bills scheduled for debate and vote in the house. These are available in print at the legislative library and online at the TLO website for recent sessions.

Figure 7-3. Bill Analysis

BILL ANALYSIS

H.B. 2766

By: Eiland
Judiciary
Committee Report (Unamended)

BACKGROUND AND PURPOSE

In Hartford, Hereford and Hampshire, hurricanes hardly happen. However, on the Gulf coast, they are unsurprising. The purpose of this bill is to permit certain courts to operate away from their ordinary locations following a natural disaster.

Currently, District and County courts are only allowed to hold court or trials in the county seat. In the case of a major hurricane the county seat may not be habitable or under mandatory evacuation orders. In order to establish a successful disaster recovery plan coastal counties need to have the ability to hold court outside the county seat during the time of displacement.

HB 2766 would allow first and second tier coastal counties to hold court outside their county seat in the event of a natural disaster.

RULEMAKING AUTHORITY

It is the committee's opinion that this bill does not expressly grant any additional rulemaking authority to a state officer, department, agency, or institution.

ANALYSIS

The bill would amend the Government Code to adding provisions that would allow presiding judges for district courts, county courts, statutory county courts and statutory probate courts to designate alternate places in certain coastal counties for the conduct of court proceedings following a natural or other major disaster in those counties.

EFFECTIVE DATE

Immediately on receipt of required vote; otherwise September 1, 2007.

---

7. Floor Debates

Bills recommended favorably by a committee proceed to the chamber to be scheduled for floor debate and vote. Unlike the practice in the U.S. Congress, there are no regularly printed records of house or senate debates. Since 1973, the debates have been recorded and are available

Figure 7-4. Fiscal Note

Local Government Impact
LEGISLATIVE BUDGET BOARD
Austin, Texas
FISCAL NOTE, 80TH LEGISLATIVE REGULAR SESSION
April 25, 2007

TO: Honorable Jeff Wentworth, Chair, Senate Committee on Jurisprudence

FROM: John S. O'Brien, Director, Legislative Budget Board

IN RE: HB2766 by Eiland (Relating to the location at which certain courts may conduct proceedings following certain disasters.), As Engrossed

No significant fiscal implication to the State is anticipated.

The bill would amend the Government Code to authorize the presiding judge of the administrative judicial region to designate an alternate location in the district at which a district court may conduct its proceedings if the district court in a "first tier" or "second tier" coastal county is unable to conduct its proceedings in a county seat due to a natural or other major disaster. The presiding judge of the administrative judicial region may also make a designation for a statutory county court, a county court, or a statutory probate court, located in a first tier or second tier coastal county in the same circumstance to conduct proceedings elsewhere.

The bill would take effect immediately if it were to receive the required two-thirds vote in each house; otherwise, it would take effect September 1, 2007.

The fiscal impact to the affected courts would vary depending on how many proceedings and accompanying records must be moved and any associated expenses; however, it is anticipated the costs would be less than if all proceedings were delayed. There may also be expenses to the courts in which the displaced courts must share courtrooms.

Source Agencies: 212 Office of Court Administration, Texas Judicial Council
LBB Staff: JOB, MN, DB

---

on tape through the house and senate media offices. Video broadcasts of floor debates since 2001 are available on the TLO website.

8. Conference Committee Reports

If a conference committee agrees on reconciled language, the amended bill is reported to each chamber with a recommendation that it be enacted. The bill markup, showing language crossed out and language added, is a useful indication of the issues addressed by the committee. See Figure 7-5 for an example of a conference committee report, with a portion of the bill markup (new language is underlined).

9. House and Senate Journals

The portion of a conference committee report in Figure 7-5 was copied from the House Journal for the date May 26, 2007. Journals of the House and Senate record the activity of the legislature during each day it is in session. The activities recorded are the readings of bills; the occurrence of floor debates; recommendations of amendments; the taking and records of votes; parliamentary questions; proclamations by the governor; messages from the other chamber; and other procedural events of the day.

In general, there is little reference to the substance of floor debates or other discussion. Evidence of legislative intent does sometimes appear in the journals, however. Particularly in the last days of the session, conference committee reports containing bill reconciliation markup may be printed in full. At times, the member presenting the report will be asked to answer a question about legislative intent from the floor. These comments may be ordered printed. Similarly, last minute changes or additions to conference committee reported bills may be introduced under waiver of regular rules as privileged resolutions. Additions proposed for vote often are followed by an explanation by the committee of the reason for the addition.

Journals also contain indexes of bills filed during the session of the legislature. These can be helpful for finding information about bills that did not become law. Bills that did not become law may still be needed for legislative history research, since many successful bills were preceded by unsuccessful attempts to pass legislation on the same matter in earlier sessions or had companion or similar bills in the same session. The documents produced during the consideration of those bills may cast light on the intent of the legislature as it considered the matter.

Figure 7-5. Conference Committee Report

HB 1594 – ADOPTION OF CONFERENCE COMMITTEE REPORT

Representative Zerwas submitted the following conference committee report on HB 1594:

Austin, Texas, May 24, 2007

The Honorable David Dewhurst
President of the Senate

The Honorable Tom Craddick
Speaker of the House of Representatives

Sirs: We, your conference committee, appointed to adjust the differences between the senate and the house of representatives on HB 1594 have had the same under consideration, and beg to report it back with the recommendation that it do pass in the form and text hereto attached.

Carona	Zerwas
Nelson	Eiland
Van de Putte	Hancock
	Martinez
	Smithee
On the part of the senate	On the part of the house

HB 1594, A bill to be entitled An Act relating to expedited credentialing for certain physicians providing services under a managed care plan.

BE IT ENACTED BY THE LEGISLATURE OF THE STATE OF TEXAS:
SECTION 1. Chapter 1452, Insurance Code, is amended by adding Subchapter C to read as follows:
SUBCHAPTER C. EXPEDITED CREDENTIALING PROCESS
FOR CERTAIN PHYSICIANS
Sec. 1452.101. DEFINITIONS. In this subchapter:
(1) "Applicant physician" means a physician applying for expedited credentialing under this subchapter.

---

10. Other Materials

Other information of various sorts might also be useful. The governor sometimes appoints interim committees to consider and report on issues during the period between sessions of the legislature. The

Table 7-3. Legislative Summary in *Vernon's*

Acts 1977, 65th Leg., p. 2420, ch. 871, art. I, §1, eff. Sept. 1, 1977. Amended by Acts 1983, 68th Leg., p. 5243, ch. 965, §3, eff. June 19, 1983; Acts 1987, 70th Leg., ch. 208, §5, eff. Aug. 31, 1987.

Source: *Vernon's Texas Statutes and Codes Annotated*. Reprinted with permission of Thomson Reuters.

reports of interim committees may contain useful information about legislation introduced and considered during the next session. The research arms of the House and Senate and the Texas Legislative Council produce reports containing legal, policy, and factual information about pending or potential legislation. The Legislative Reference Library of Texas prepares the *List of Sections Affected*, indicating the sections or articles of subject codes, the Revised Civil Statutes, or independent codes that would be affected by pending bills.

B. Preparing a Texas Legislative History: Print and Online Resources

The researcher preparing a Texas legislative history will typically use a combination of print and online sources, as well as audio files. At each step of the research process, choose the more convenient online resources, if they are available. If the resources are not online, the print sources must be sought. The most important thing is to understand the steps of the process and the resources that are available at each step.

1. Locate the Act in the Session Laws

At the end of each statutory section or article in *Vernon's* is a summary of the original legislation and all subsequent amending legislation that created that section in its current form. See Table 7-3 for an example.

A legislative summary cite gives the year and legislative session, the chapter (recall that enacted laws are published as "chapters" in the *General and Special Laws of the State of Texas*), the section in the session law chapter containing the language for this section or article of the subject code, Revised Civil Statutes, or independent code and the date on which the statute became effective. The goal is to locate the act that added the language in question. Sometimes a historical note immediately following the summary gives considerable detail about the original act and the changes introduced by amending acts. The note might direct the researcher to the act for which legislative history must be found. Otherwise, the researcher will start by studying the most recent amending act and work back through successively earlier acts until the act adding the language is found. To gain adequate context, it may also be necessary to examine the earlier acts, especially the originating act, in the *General and Special Laws of the State of Texas*. The session laws are available in many law libraries, either in print or in the session laws collection of HeinOnline.

2. Note the Bill Number and Legislative Session

For each act for which a legislative history is needed, locate in the session laws the volume for the legislative session and the chapter. After reading the relevant sections, note in your research journal the bill number and the session in which it was passed. The bill number (e.g., H.B. 4, S.B. 23) is assigned when the bill is introduced in the House or Senate and is the number by which the bill and all related documents are identified as the bill passes through the legislative process. A house bill number, for example, is the number used for all documents and actions as a bill progresses through the House, the Senate, and the final stages of enactment.

Alternatively, the researcher can use the online Legislative Archive System of the Legislative Reference Library. Searching the "Direct search" page[6] by chapter number yields a page with bill number, bill history and information, and some documents. The TLO site, discussed earlier, often contains more documents, however. Record the bill number and use it to search the TLO site, at www.legis.state.tx.us. This online approach is usually more convenient than using the session law volumes.

---

6. The address is www.lrl.state.tx.us/legis/billsearch/lrlhome.cfm.

3. Examine the Bill File

Official documents developed during the legislative process are collected in the bill file. The bill file contains versions of the bill, fiscal notes, bill analyses, witness lists, committee minutes, and committee reports, as well as a brief history of the bill's passage through the process and a list of the documents that should be in the bill file. The year 1973 saw substantial legislative reform in Texas. Bill files from the years before 1973 may or may not contain bill analyses and other supporting documentation. The bill file will not contain transcripts of committee hearings or floor debates; these are available only on audio tape or in video.

The format in which the bill file is available depends on the year in which a bill was enacted. Bill files for bills enacted prior to 1943 (48th legislature) are available only in print at the Texas State Library in Austin. The Legislative Reference Library of Texas website contains an archive of scanned bill files from 1943 to 2001 (77th legislature). To access the archive, go to www.lrl.state.tx.us and click on "Legislative Archive System."

The TLO website contains bill file documents in PDF and word-processing formats for the years 1993 (73rd session) to present. To get these documents, use "Bill Lookup" or the quick search feature on the TLO home page to search by session and bill number. The record contains several tabs. The History tab contains a full history of the bill and related information. The Text tab has downloadable files of the documents from the bill file.

The researcher wishing to examine the original bill file can get bill files in print at the Legislative Reference Library of Texas for sessions from 1973 to present.

4. Listen to Audio Tapes of Committee Hearings and Floor Debates

The testimony and discussion during committee hearings may cast light on legislative intent. It is important to remember that the witnesses and, often, the legislators are acting as advocates and may be in adversarial roles, so the context of the discussions must be carefully considered. Researchers also often look to the statements and debates of legislators on the floor of the House or Senate. Statements on the floor may also reflect advocacy and adversarial positions. The degree to which particular statements represent the intent of the legislature as a whole must be carefully considered in light of the context.

Records of committee hearings and floor debates are available on audio tape. To locate the recordings, first obtain a list of actions on the bill. Bill histories are available on the TLO website from 1989 (71st session) to present. For 1973 through 1989 (63rd session through 71st session), bill histories are available online from the Legislative Research Library website at www.lrl.state.tx.us. For histories of bills before 1973, the House and Senate journals must be used.

5. Consider Other Documents

Other sources might provide information about legislative intent. The House and Senate journals sometimes contain statements by sponsors or committee members indicating legislative intent, often in response to questions from other members. In fact, statements are sometimes headed "Statement of Legislative Intent." The House and Senate journals are held by many libraries. Journals from 1995 (74th legislature) are available at the house website at www.journals.house.state.tx.us/hjrnl/home.htm and from 1999 (76th legislature) on the senate website at www.journals.senate.state.tx.us/sjrnl/home.htm. Daily Floor Reports, containing analyses of selected bills, have been prepared by the House Research Organization since 1975. Reports from 1995 are available on the HRO website at www.hro.house.state.tx.us/FloorReport.aspx. The researcher might find other reports by interim committees, the House Research Organization, Senate Research Center, and other state agencies and commissions on their websites.

C. Texas Legislative History on Westlaw and LexisNexis

Westlaw and LexisNexis each have some Texas legislative history material available. Since these collections are less complete and cover fewer years than those available online from the State of Texas, the researcher is usually better off working with the free, state-supplied materials. On Westlaw, use database TX-LH. On LexisNexis, use database "Texas Legislative Bill History." Be sure to check the scope notes before searching.

V. Federal Legislative History Research

The process of federal legislative history research is generally similar to that for Texas. Begin by finding the relevant section of the United States Code (U.S.C.). The legislative summary at the end of the section lists the original public law that created the language of the section and any subsequent amending public laws. When bills are enacted by the United States Congress, they are given a public law number. The public law number is in the form P.L. sss-nnn, with the number before the hyphen indicating the session and the number after the hyphen representing the chronological order of enactment during the session. Once the public law number is identified, a copy of the public law can be found in several sources.

The public law is originally published as a "slip law." It is eventually published with the other public laws of the session in a volume or volumes of the official publication, *Statutes at Large*. Since new volumes of the *Statutes at Large* are slow to appear, public laws have historically been made available soon after publication in the commercially published *United States Code Congressional and Administrative News* (U.S.C.C.A.N.), a West publication. Sets of U.S.C.C.A.N. are widely available in libraries. Since the Thomas website was established in 1995, the texts of public laws have appeared online very soon after enactment. Thomas contains the text of enrolled bills or public laws from 1989 (101st Congress) to present. The researcher should use the most convenient source of public laws in order to obtain the number of the bill that became the public law. The bill number is included on the first page of every public law. As in Texas, the bill number stays with the bill throughout its legislative progress and is used to identify all documents developed during the process.

A. Sources of Federal Legislative History

The stages of the federal legislative process are similar to those in Texas. The documents developed at each stage, however, differ somewhat from those in Texas in their availability, degree of detail, and the importance given to them.

Floor debate in the U.S. House of Representatives and U.S. Senate is printed in the *Congressional Record*, unlike Texas, where only audio tapes and some video recordings are available. Although the debates are published, they must be used with caution. Congressmen and senators can amend their remarks before publication, or even add remarks not actually delivered on the floor. Such later additions are generally marked by different typefaces or signals in the *Congressional Record*. Check to see how the volume you are using indicates remarks added after the floor debate.

Committee work is also central to the federal legislative process. Congressional committee reports are very influential legislative history documents. Unlike the often summary recommendations and markups of Texas committee reports, United States House and Senate committee reports contain detailed discussion of background and policy and section by section explanation of the meaning and policies of the bill. Of lesser importance are the committee prints, the factual and statistical analyses prepared by research staff as the "homework" of the committee. Transcripts are available for many committee hearings and testimony, although transcripts also rank lower in influence than committee reports.

The most influential documents of all are conference committee reports, for interpreting those parts of a public law drafted by the conferees as they negotiated differences between the bill versions of the two chambers.

A type of document that is often included in legislative histories is the "signing statement" by the President, in which the President may state his interpretation of the public law or his intent as to its administration and enforcement. The status of presidential signing statements is much debated.

B. Compiling a Federal Legislative History

The researcher in federal legislative history is fortunate to have much of the work already done, in many cases. For all federal public laws since 1969, complete legislative histories have been prepared and published by the Congressional Information Service (C.I.S.). The *CIS Index and Abstracts* series and associated legislative history volumes provide for each public law abstracts of documents and cites to Superintendent of Documents (SuDoc) numbers and C.I.S. numbers. The SuDoc number allows documents to be obtained from government depositories or collections of microfiche documents held by many law libraries. The C.I.S. number can be used to locate a document in the microfiche set published by C.I.S. as a companion to the indexes. The C.I.S. indexes and microfiche are held by many law libraries. The complete C.I.S. indexes and the full-text documents from about 1990 to present are available online through the ProQuest *Congressional* database. Many law libraries subscribe to ProQuest *Congressional*.

Legislative histories have been compiled for many public laws. Some of these are comprehensive compilations of legislative history documents. The researcher with access to a law library should check the library catalog for compiled legislative histories. Some document compilations are also available on Westlaw and LexisNexis. Other compiled legislative histories are simply lists of the documents produced during the legislative process. Appendix B contains titles of books that have collected cites to compiled legislative histories on various topics.

In recent years, many of the documents needed for federal legislative history research have been made available on Thomas and on FDsys. For years preceding the start of the C.I.S. legislative history series in 1969, brief legislative histories and selected committee reports are widely available in U.S.C.C.A.N., which began publication in 1942 under the title *United State Code Congressional Service*. Research into the legislative histories of earlier public laws is more challenging. The *CIS US Congressional Committee Hearings Index* can be used to identify committee hearings for the years 1833 to 1969. These can be requested from Government Printing Office depository libraries.

Chapter 8

Administrative Law

I. Overview

The preceding chapters of this book have dealt mostly with research in the law created by legislatures and courts. Legislation and judicial decisions, reflecting the structure of the governments established by the U.S. and Texas constitutions, were the predominant sources of law early in U.S. and Texas history. As society became more complex and the view of government's role in society expanded, the need arose to develop institutions to regulate many parts of society in ways that were beyond the capacities of legislatures and the court system. The solution at the federal and state levels was the development of administrative agencies.

Administrative agencies go by many names, such as board, commission, agency, or office. An administrative agency is an executive body, in that its responsibility is to execute the mandate of the legislature regarding some area of social activity. The authority to exercise governmental powers must be formally delegated to the agency by the legislature. The delegation of authority is done by an "enabling statute" or a constitutional provision that establishes the agency, identifies its responsibilities, and declares the extent and nature of the powers delegated.

The typical agency exercises powers that are legislative, judicial, and executive in nature. Although sometimes called "quasi-legislative" or "quasi-judicial," the actions of agencies result in law just as mandatory to those affected as law created by the legislature or courts. In fact, the law created by administrative agencies is the law individuals and organizations deal with most of the time. The law created and administered by agencies is the primary concern of many lawyers.

Table 8-1. Example of the Relationship Between a Statute and Rules

A Texas statute provides that the Texas Department of Public safety shall adopt rules to administer a subchapter relating to license denial, suspension, or revocation.

The Texas Department of Public Safety promulgated a rule under the authority of the statute, providing:

> The department will cancel a drivers license upon confirmation of any of the following:
>
> (1) nonpayment of fee;
> (2) all applicants suspended in another state;
> (3) death of authorizing signer;
> (4) withdrawal of authorization for a minor;
> (5) mental incapacity;
> (6) some false statement convictions;
> (7) failure to complete a concurrent driver education course;
> (8) license issued to a person not entitled thereto.

Sources: *Texas Transportation Code* § 521.291; 37 *Texas Administrative Code* § 15.87.

The agency activity analogous to legislation is "rule making." Rules, sometimes called "regulations," are much more detailed than the legislation authorizing them, since they apply the broad mandates of the legislation to the many activities of a complex society. See Table 8-1 for an example of the relationship between statutes and rules. Agencies also perform internal executive functions. Agencies monitor compliance with their rules and formulate internal policies, guidelines, and procedures for enforcing their rules. The judicial functions of the agency are the adjudication of disputes regarding violations of rules, or such actions as rate making or the issuance of licenses. Adjudications are proceedings much like trials. They are held before "administrative law judges" (A.L.J.s), who decide the disputes and issue written opinions. There may be a right of appeal of the A.L.J. decision to a higher authority within the agency. Once the appeals process has been exhausted within the agency, the parties typically may appeal the agency's final order to the state or federal courts.

Table 8-2. Outline for Texas Administrative Law Research

1. Find the enabling act or section of the Texas Constitution granting the agency power to act. Research case law to determine whether the agency acted within the scope of its delegated power.
2. Find the relevant rule in the *Texas Administrative Code* for the year at issue. The T.A.C. online is continually updated as final rules are published.
3. Check the *Texas Register* to see if any proposed rules may affect the issue.
4. Find agency and judicial decisions to see how the rule is applied and interpreted.

II. Texas Administrative Law Research

Administrative law research primarily involves locating the enabling act or constitutional provision granting power to the agency, finding rules promulgated by the agency, and finding A.L.J. decisions and decisions by the courts. Often, researchers also need to seek information about internal policies, guidelines, and procedures of the agency. Table 8-2 lists the steps of the administrative law research process.

A. Researching the Enabling Act

Since the authority of administrative agencies is established in a constitutional provision or by the legislature in an enabling act, the first analytical step is to determine whether an agency acted within the scope of its delegated power. If this is in doubt, use techniques discussed in Chapter 3 on constitutions or in Chapter 6 on statutory research to find the constitutional provision or enabling act. The next step is to locate cases interpreting the relevant parts of the provision or enabling act using the techniques discussed in Chapter 5 on researching judicial opinions.

Table 8-3. Example of Numbering of *Texas Administrative Code*

The *Texas Administrative Code* is organized by numbered "titles." Each title is divided into numbered "parts." Each part is divided into numbered "chapters." A chapter may be divided into "subchapters." Subchapters are divided into "sections," the level at which the text of rules appears. The following example shows the hierarchy from a title down to a particular section:

Title 37. Public Safety and Corrections
 Part I. Texas Department of Public Safety
  Chapter 1. Organization and Administration
   Subchapter A. Objective, Mission, and Program
    Section 1.1 Broad Objective

Source: *Texas Administration Code* (2008). Reprinted with permission of Thomson Reuters.

B. Finding Texas Agency Rules

Texas administrative agencies are in the executive branch, under the authority of the governor. The activities of agencies are controlled by the Administrative Procedure and Texas Register Act (A.P.T.R.A. or A.P.A.).[1] The A.P.T.R.A. requires publication in the *Texas Register* of notice of proposed rules, including opportunities for public participation and comment on proposed rules, and notice of adopted rules. The *Texas Register*, published weekly, also includes emergency rules; notice that rules that have been withdrawn; proclamations, appointments, and executive orders by the governor; notices of requests for attorney general opinions; summaries of attorney general opinions; and other public notices required by statute. The *Texas Register* is available online at www.sos.state.tx.us/texreg/index.shtml. Archives of the *Texas Register* are maintained by the University of North Texas at http://texinfo.library.unt.edu/texasregister.

Final rules are codified in the *Texas Administrative Code* (T.A.C.). Some numbers are not included in the sequence of titles; these numbers are reserved for expansion. See Table 8-3 for an example of the

---

1. Administrative Procedure and Texas Register Act, 64th Leg., R.S., ch. 61, 1975 Tex. Gen. Law 136 (currently codified at Tex. Gov't Code Ann. §§ 2001.001–.902 (West 2008 & Supp. 2011)).

numbering of Texas administrative rules. The T.A.C. is codified and updated by the secretary of state and printed by West. A continually updated T.A.C. is available online at www.sos.state.tx.us/tac/index.shtml. The T.A.C. and *Texas Register* are available on Westlaw and LexisNexis in their Texas administrative law collections.

1. *Find Sections in the* Texas Administrative Code

The researcher might find cites to T.A.C. sections while reading secondary sources in the early stages of the research process. These cites should be investigated, but thorough research in the primary authorities is still necessary.

Each rule published in the *Texas Register* contains a statement of the statutory authority under which the rule was promulgated. Figure 8-1 shows a brief adopted rule. If there had been public comments and the text of the rule had been printed, the publication announcing the adopted rule would have been longer. Note the references to the statutory authority for the rule and the statement that the rule is within the authority of the agency. The researcher using online versions of the *Texas Register*, such as the site maintained by the state or on Westlaw or LexisNexis, can find the sections of the T.A.C. promulgated under the authority of a particular statutory section by doing a word search using the name of the subject code or Revised Civil Statute title and the section or article number.[2]

Searches by section or article number might not turn up all relevant rules. The author of the note might have overlooked an authority or cited it slightly differently. Thus, searches using the finding tools provided in the T.A.C. should also be conducted.

The final volume of the T.A.C. contains the index. Review the index for the search terms developed during the research process, and

---

2. Since rules can only be promulgated under delegated authority, and the researcher usually begins primary law research in the statutes, it would be very useful to have finding tools listing the rules promulgated under the authority of particular statutory sections or articles. A finding tool indicating which rules relate to which statutory sections exists for federal regulatory research, but not for Texas rules.

Figure 8-1. Adopted Rule in *Texas Register*

PART 14.   TEXAS OPTOMETRY BOARD

CHAPTER 280.   THERAPEUTIC OPTOMETRY

22 TAC §280.7

The Texas Optometry Board adopts the repeal of §280.7 without changes to the proposed text published in the December 1, 2006, issue of the *Texas Register* (31 TexReg 9677).

The rule concerns the Optometric Health Care Advisory Committee, which was abolished by §351.165 of the Optometry Act on September 1, 2005.

No comments were received.

The repeal of §280.7 is adopted under the Texas Optometry Act, Texas Occupations Code, §351.151 and §351.165.

No other sections are affected by this repeal.

The Texas Optometry Board interprets §351.151 as authorizing the adoption of procedural and substantive rules for the regulation of the optometric profession. The Board interprets §351.165 as creating the Optometric Health Care Advisory Committee, and setting a date of September 1, 2005, to abolish the Committee.

This agency hereby certifies that the adoption has been reviewed by legal counsel and found to be a valid exercise of the agency's legal authority.

Filed with the Office of the Secretary of State on February 28, 2007.

TRD-200700792

Source: *Texas Register* (2007).

be sure to follow up on any cross-references. Also, check the tables of contents of titles appearing relevant to the subject being researched. Read the rules found by these searches carefully and check surrounding rules to see if they are relevant. At the end of each section in the T.A.C. is a source note telling when the rule became effective and giving the *Texas Register* cite for its original publication. Be sure to read source notes and make a note of the *Texas Register* cite. Accompanying the adopted rule published in the *Texas Register* are statements concerning agency policy and explanations why various public comments were or were not reflected in the final rule. These statements by the agency may be useful in understanding the rule or in persuading a court to adopt a particular interpretation.

2. Use the Texas Register

In the days before the T.A.C. was available in constantly updated form online, it was necessary to update the results of searches in the T.A.C. by searching the *Texas Register* for rules promulgated subsequent to the most recent T.A.C. print publication. This method of updating is no longer necessary for Texas administrative rule research. The *Texas Register* is still necessary for several research purposes, however.

First, the researcher often needs to know if new rules have been proposed that may affect client interests or particular areas of law. Many researchers make a habit of checking every new issue of the *Texas Register* for new proposed rules. Next, the *Texas Register* contains emergency rules. These are in effect for only limited times and are not included in the T.A.C. The *Texas Register* also includes withdrawn rules. Knowing that proposed rules have been withdrawn is important if the proposed rule is being tracked. Also, rules that have been proposed and withdrawn might cast light on agency initiatives that finally led to promulgated final rules, or otherwise inform about agency policies and history.

3. Review the Agency Website

Agency websites sometimes contain information about regulatory agendas, proposed rules, opportunities for comment and public hearings, final rules, and other useful information. The researcher specializing in an area of regulatory law will need to become familiar with the agency website. Often the best sources of agency information are the people at the agency. Contact information are available at the agency website and in the *Texas State Directory*. In addition, email notification of actions by an agency can be subscribed to by contacting the office of the *Texas Register*.

Table 8-4. Texas Agencies with Regularly Published Decisions

Texas Comptroller of Public Accounts Hearing Decisions
Texas Public Utilities Commission Decisions
Texas State Securities Board; Opinions and Decisions
Texas Workers' Compensation Decisions

C. Finding Texas Agency Decisions

Agencies adjudicate contested matters regarding non-compliance with rules, granting of licenses, and other matters within their jurisdiction. The first stage of dealing with such matters within an agency is often an informal discussion with an agency reviewing officer. If a matter cannot be resolved informally, the next stage is typically a formal hearing before an A.L.J. These adjudications are much like trials in the state court system, with each party having a right to counsel and adherence to court rules governing procedure and evidence.

The opinion of the A.L.J. is published as a printed "agency decision." It is necessary to search for agency decisions to see how the agency has interpreted and applied its rules. Some Texas agencies report their agency opinions in regular publications or online. Table 8-4 lists agencies with regularly published agency decisions. Check the website of an agency to see whether agency opinions are posted online. Westlaw and LexisNexis have the publications of some Texas agencies in their Texas administrative law collections.

Since 1991, adjudications before A.L.J.s have been performed for many state agencies by the Texas State Office of Administrative Hearings (S.O.A.H.). The opinion of an S.O.A.H. administrative law judge is issued as a "proposal for decision" (P.F.D.).[3] The P.F.D. includes discussion of issues and evidence presented, findings of fact, conclusions of law, and recommendations for agency action. The agency must adopt the P.F.D. for a final decision and order to issue.

---

3. For a few types of hearings, the S.O.A.H. issues final orders and decisions. See the S.O.A.H. FAQs webpage, at www.soah.state.tx.us/AboutUs/faq.htm, for specifics.

Copies of P.F.D.s are available at the S.O.A.H. website, at www.soah.state.tx.us, where they may be searched by agency name or code, S.O.A.H. docket number, keywords, and time span within which the P.F.D. was issued. Transcripts of hearings can also be obtained from the S.O.A.H.

D. Appeals from Agency Decisions

A right of appeal from the decision of the A.L.J. to a higher administrative authority within the agency may exist. Once a final order has been issued and the remedies within the agency are exhausted, there is typically a right to appeal the decision to a Texas district court. The adjudicative powers of the agency are established by the agency's enabling statute, as are details of any right to judicial review of agency opinions. If the enabling statute provides for internal adjudication and judicial review, the Texas A.P.A. governs the procedures to be followed. Refer to the enabling statute to determine whether an agency's actions are within the authority granted by statute. Actions outside of agency authority may be challenged in the Texas courts. Otherwise, there is no right of judicial review of agency decisions under Texas law, unless a statute provides a right of appeal, the agency order affects a vested property right, or the order violates a constitutional right.[4]

Search for appellate court cases citing Texas rules using the techniques discussed in Chapter 5. The online citators, Westlaw's KeyCite and LexisNexis' Shepard's, can also be used to locate cases citing Texas rules.

III. Federal Administrative Law Research

Federal administrative agencies are formed in much the same way and perform similar functions as Texas agencies. They are established

---

4. *Gen. Servs. Comm'n v. Little-Tex Insulation, Co., Inc.*, 39 S.W.3d 591, 599 (Tex. 2001).

and delegated authority by enabling acts. Federal agencies engage in rule making, monitor and enforce compliance, and adjudicate disputes. They have A.L.J.s and operate under the federal Administrative Procedure Act (A.P.A.).[5] There is generally a right to appeal to the federal courts from final decisions and orders. The scope of agency authority, internal organization and procedures, and rights of judicial review are governed by the enabling acts. Be sure to examine the enabling acts in order to assess whether an agency is operating within the bounds of its authority and to pursue the proper avenues for remedies.

A. Finding Federal Agency Regulations

Rules from federal administrative agencies are often called "regulations." Federal agency regulations are published in a scheme similar to that described for Texas.

Agencies must publish notice of proposed rules[6] in the *Federal Register*, published every business day. The notice provides a statement of the proposed rule and its purpose, solicits comments, and indicates how and to whom comments are to be submitted. If the agency promulgates a final rule after consideration of public comments, the final rule is published in the *Federal Register*, together with discussion of comments received, how they were considered, explanation of the policy and meaning of the rule, and the date the rule takes effect. The statutory authority under which the rule is promulgated is also included in the notices.

Agency rules are codified in the *Code of Federal Regulations* (C.F.R.), consisting of fifty subject titles. The C.F.R. is so vast that it is updated

---

5. 5 U.S.C. §§ 551–59 (2006).

6. The *Federal Register* uses the terms "proposed rule" and "final rule" in its rule-making notices, even though the final rules are codified in a publication called the *Code of Federal Regulations*. The terms "rule" and "regulation" are often popularly used as synonyms or combined, as in "rules and regulations." In Texas, the term "rule" is fixed by statutory definition, and thus is the form generally used.

Figure 8-2. C.F.R. Parallel Table

CFR Index

1 U.S.C.	CFR
112	1 Part 2
112a—112b	22 Part 181
113	1 Part 2
133	32 Part 151
2 U.S.C.	
136	36 Parts 701—703, 705
170	36 Part 705
179	36 Part 704
215	38 Parts 49
431—432	11 Parts 104, 110, 114
431	11 Parts 100, 109, 400
432—434	11 Part 102
432	11 Parts 101, 103, 105, 111, 113
433—434	11 Part 116
434	11 Parts 100, 101, 104, 105, 108, 109, 114, 300, 400, 9006
437	11 Parts 107, 9008
437d	11 Parts 110, 111, 113, 114, 115, 200, 201
437f—437g	11 Part 5
437f	11 Parts 112, 201
437g	11 Part 111
438	11 Parts 5, 100—109, 110, 111—116, 200, 201, 300, 400, 9008
439	11 Part 108
439a	11 Parts 104, 113
441a—441b	11 Parts 110, 116
441a	11 Parts 104, 106, 109 113, 300, 400
441a–1	11 Part 109
441b	11 Part 114
441d—441h	11 Parts 109, 110
441d	11 Parts 102, 109
441i	11 Parts 300, 9008
	34 Part 73
451	11 Part 16
453	11 Parts 108, 300
901	31 Parts 317, 321
1351	29 Parts 457—459

5 U.S.C.—Continued	CFR
500	28 Part 79
	29 Parts 103, 580
	31 Parts 8, 10
	37 Part 10
501	28 Part 9
	41 Part 114-52
503	29 Part 580
504	5 Parts 2430, 2610
	7 Part 1
	10 Part 12
	12 Parts 19, 263, 308, 509, 509b, 625, 1735
	13 Part 134
	14 Parts 14, 1262
	15 Part 18
	16 Part 1025
	17 Part 148
	19 Part 212
	22 Part 134
	24 Part 14
	28 Part 24
	29 Parts 16, 102, 2204, 2704
	31 Part 6
	34 Part 21
	39 Part 960
	43 Part 4
	45 Part 13
	46 Part 502
	49 Parts 826, 1016
522	17 Part 3
	26 Part 301
	37 Part 302
522b	17 Part 3
551 *et seq*	14 Parts 201, 211
	16 Part 1025
	18 Parts 281, 286
	32 Parts 202

Source: *Code of Federal Regulations* (2008).

in four batches each year, so that at any time some titles have been recently updated, while others may not have been updated for a full year.

The research process will often start in secondary authority in order to understand the agency and regulatory regime for the area being researched. The next step is to perform statutory research to find the controlling parts of the United States Code. It is then necessary to determine which regulations have been promulgated under the authority of controlling statutes. The annotations in the U.S.C.A. and U.S.C.S. (see Chapter 6) often identify regulations promulgated under the authority of a section of the U.S.C.

Even more useful is the parallel table in the index volume of the C.F.R. See Figure 8-2 for a page of the C.F.R. parallel table. In the page of the parallel table shown, the right-hand side of a column gives

Figure 8-3. C.F.R. Index Page

CFR Index	Chemicals
Central Security Service *See* National Security Agency/Central Security Service **Cereals (commodity)** *See* Grains **Cereals (food)** Cereal flours and related products, 21 CFR 137 **Cervids** Chronic wasting disease control, 9 CFR 55 Chronic wasting disease in deer, elk and moose, 9 CFR 81 **Chaplains** Army Department, 32 CFR 510 **Charitable contributions** Solicitation of Federal civilian and uniformed services personnel for contributions to private voluntary organizations, 5 CFR 950 **Charter buses** *See* Buses **Charter flights** Canadian charter air taxi operators, 14 CFR 294 Certification and operations Air carriers and commercial operators, 14 CFR 119	Banks, banking **Cheese** Antidumping and countervailing duties, quota cheese subsidy, 19 CFR 351 Food grades and standards, 21 CFR 133 Import quotas and fees, 7 CFR 6 **Chemical Safety and Hazard Investigation Board** Administrative investigations, 40 CFR 1610 Federal Tort Claims Act, administrative claims, 40 CFR 1620 Government in the Sunshine Act, rules implementing, 40 CFR 1603 Legal proceedings Employees testimony, 40 CFR 1611 Records production, 40 CFR 1612 Organization and functions, 40 CFR 1600 Privacy and access to individual records, protection under 1974 Privacy Act, 40 CFR 1602 Records disclosure procedures under Freedom of Information Act, 40 CFR 1601 **Chemicals** *See also* Specific chemicals; Drugs; Fertilizers; Hazardous substances; Pesticides and pests

Source: *Code of Federal Regulations* (2008).

the C.F.R. cites of the regulations promulgated under the authority of the U.S.C. sections cited in the left-hand side of that column.

The annotations and the parallel table are very useful, but it sometimes happens that they do not identify all relevant regulations. The researcher must also search the index volume using the search terms developed in the research process. The C.F.R. index is organized both by agency name and by alphabetized search terms; be sure to look both under the agency name and in the general list of terms. Figure 8-3 is a page from the C.F.R. index.

Be sure to check the authority note of every rule found by using the C.F.R. index to see if there is statutory authority not discovered in previous research steps. See Figure 8-4 for a page from the C.F.R. The authority note is right after the heading for each section. Following the authority note is a source note, indicating where the rule

Figure 8-4. Page from the *Code of Federal Regulations*

§ 314.111(a)(5)(ii) of this chapter.

*   *   *   *   *

PART 203—PRESCRIPTION DRUG MARKETING

Subpart A—General Provisions

Sec.
203.1 Scope.
203.2 Purpose.
203.3 Definitions.

Subpart B—Reimportation

203.10 Restrictions on reimportation.
203.11 Applications for reimportation to provide emergency medical care.
203.12 An appeal from an adverse decision by the district office.

Subpart C—Sales Restrictions

203.20 Sales restrictions.
203.22 Exclusions.
203.23 Returns.

Subpart D—Samples

203.30 Sample distribution by mail or common carrier.
203.31 Sample distribution by means other than mail or common carrier (direct delivery by a representative or detailer).

AUTHORITY: 21 U.S.C. 331, 333, 351, 352, 353, 360, 371, 374, 381.

SOURCE: 64 FR 67756, Dec. 3, 1999, unless otherwise noted.

Subpart A—General Provisions

§ 203.1 Scope.

This part sets forth procedures and requirements pertaining to the reimportation and wholesale distribution of prescription drugs, including both bulk drug substances and finished dosage forms; the sale, purchase, or trade of (or the offer to sell, purchase, or trade) prescription drugs, including bulk drug substances, that were purchased by hospitals or health care entities, or donated to charitable organizations; and the distribution of prescription drug samples. Blood and blood components intended for transfusion are excluded from the restrictions in and the requirements of the Prescription Drug Marketing Act of 1987 and the Prescription Drug Amendments of 1992.

§ 203.2 Purpose.

The purpose of this part is to implement the Prescription Drug Marketing Act of 1987 and the Prescription Drug

103

Source: *Code of Federal Regulations* (2008).

was originally published in the *Federal Register*. Read and understand any new statutory authority discovered while searching for regulations. The subdivisions of the C.F.R. are Title, Chapter, Subchapter, Part, Subpart, and Section.

B. Updating Federal Agency Regulations

After locating relevant regulations in the C.F.R., update them by searching the *Federal Register* for rules that have been promulgated or proposed since the cutoff date for rules included in the C.F.R. volume. Updating federal regulations is not yet as easy as updating in Texas, with its continually updated T.A.C.

To update the C.F.R., whether in print or online, it is necessary to use a tool called the *List of CFR Sections Affected* (L.S.A.). Start by locating the most recent L.S.A. volume. In print, this volume will be located just after the C.F.R. set. Look up the agency, then the C.F.R. section number, and see if the C.F.R. section is listed. If it is, the five-digit number after it is the page number in the *Federal Register* for the year where the notice is published (the *Federal Register* is paginated consecutively through the entire year). Next, find the last *Federal Register* for each month since the coverage of the L.S.A. supplement. Check the cumulative monthly L.S.A. at the end of the volumes just like you did in the L.S.A. supplement. Since there are several issues of the *Federal Register* that have not yet made it to the library shelves, finish by checking the most current issues online at FDsys.

The *Federal Register* and C.F.R. are available on FDsys and commercial sites such as LexisNexis, Westlaw, and HeinOnline. While Westlaw updates its C.F.R. databases to include recent regulations, the updates typically lag the publication of the *Federal Register* by about a week. A note in the header gives the issue of the C.F.R. through which the text of the regulation has been updated. It is possible vendor updating processes have missed something, and their updated version of the C.F.R. are not official. It is best to do your own updating, as described above, to be assured nothing has been missed.

C. Finding Federal Agency Decisions

Like Texas agencies, federal agencies adjudicate cases that arise under an agency's regulations. The decisions by federal agency A.L.J.s are published in official reporters by many agencies. A list of these is contained in Table T.1 of the *Bluebook*. Check the agency website to see whether an agency publishes its decisions online. Westlaw and LexisNexis also provide access to many agency decisions.

Before the Internet facilitated wide distribution of government documents, agency decisions were often difficult to locate. Commercial publishers, such as C.C.H. and B.N.A., addressed this need by gathering and publishing agency decisions for certain agencies as part of their topical looseleaf services. The decisions were gathered annually into bound reporter volumes. These commercial reporters are still often used and cited. Examples are C.C.H.'s *Occupational Safety and Health Decisions* and B.N.A.'s *Labor Relations Reference Manual.*

D. Finding Judicial Decisions Interpreting Federal Regulations

Judicial decisions interpreting agency rules or regulations are searched using the techniques of case searching discussed in Chapter 5. Westlaw and LexisNexis case databases can be searched using the techniques discussed in Chapters 2 and 5. Westlaw's KeyCite and LexisNexis' Shepard's can also be used to locate cases citing federal regulations. As in other case research, using a citator as a back-up tool for finding cases that may have been missed by other search techniques is always a good idea. See Chapter 9 Part IV. on using citators as case-finding tools.

IV. Attorney General Opinions

A. Texas Attorney General Opinions

The Attorney General of Texas is an elected official whose office performs many legal tasks for the state. Among the tasks is providing legal opinions requested by the governor or other state officials and persons listed by statute as "authorized requestors."

Attorney general opinions interpret uncertain issues of state law. There are three classes of attorney general opinions: opinions, letter opinions, and open record interpretations. "Opinions" interpret issues that may affect people or organizations throughout the state. "Letter opinions" address issues of interest only to local areas or specific persons or organizations. The attorney general stopped providing letter opinions as of January 4, 1999. "Open record interpretations" address whether a specific request for government records falls within an exception to the release of information requested under the Texas Public Information Act (formerly the Open Records Act).[7]

---

7. Tex. Gov't Code Ann. §§ 552.001–.353 (West 2004 & Supp. 2011).

Like the opinions of other legal counsel, opinions of the attorney general are advisory only. The requestors are not bound to follow the advice of an opinion. Attorney general opinions do not make law, but they are considered to be authoritative until overruled by statute or judicial decision. The courts are not bound by attorney general opinions, but do treat them as highly persuasive interpretations of Texas law.

Requests for attorney general opinions and summaries of opinions are published in the *Texas Register*. Since 1947, an index and digest of the opinions has been published annually by the Office of the Attorney General. The website of the Office of the Attorney General contains a database with all opinions since 1939, letter opinions from 1953 until their cessation in 1999, and open records opinions since 1973. The site has several research tools: simple and advanced search templates; a subject index; a database of overruled, modified, affirmed, and withdrawn opinions; and pending requests for opinions. Opinions prior to 1939 are less available. Some were issued annually in attorney general reports, but were not numbered or classified. All opinions since 1939 have been numbered. In recent years, attorney general opinion numbers begin with the initials of the sitting attorney general. For example, a recent opinion from the office of Attorney General Greg Abbott is numbered GA-0495.

B. Federal Attorney General Opinions

The United States Attorney General is appointed by the President and serves as the head of the Department of Justice (D.O.J.). The function of writing opinions is performed by the Office of Legal Counsel within the D.O.J. Opinions may only be requested by the President and certain officials in the executive branch agencies. The opinions are advisory in nature, but are considered highly persuasive by the courts.

Opinions the D.O.J. has determined are appropriate for publication have been published since 1791. The website of the Office of Legal Counsel contains a database of memoranda and opinions from 1992 to present. LexisNexis and Westlaw each have a database of the published opinions of the Office of Legal Counsel for the years from 1977 to present.

Chapter 9

Updating with Citators

I. What Citators Do: Online and Print Formats

Legal authority is constantly changing. The rules in judicial opinions are overruled, distinguished, or in other ways affected by later opinions. Statutes and regulations are amended, removed, or replaced by later legislation or rule making. All legal research must find the most current authority as the basis for analysis. The researcher must update authority throughout the research project, and the very last step in any research project is a final check to confirm that all authority cited is current. Procedures for updating statutes and administrative agency rules were discussed in Chapters 6, 7, and 8. This chapter will focus on updating research in judicial opinions. The citators discussed are Shepard's, on LexisNexis, and KeyCite, on Westlaw.

Although updating case law is the focus of this chapter, these citators also are used to identify cites to statutes, rules and regulations, administrative agency decisions, law journal articles, and other authority. The citators can thus be used to supplement and double-check updating procedures used for such resources. Coverage of these forms of authority differs from state to state and is not identical in Shepard's and KeyCite, so the coverage of a particular resource should always be checked in the citator chosen.

It is important to be clear on the terminology of updating. A "cited" authority is one whose citation has been used by a later authority as support for some point. A "citing" authority is one that uses a citation to some earlier authority as support for some point. When updating with a citator, the citation entered is the cited authority. The

Table 9-1. Outline for Updating Online

1. Access the online citator and enter the citation of the case to be updated in the box provided.
2. Select the type of citation list needed: a short list showing the direct history and negative treatment of the cited case, or a longer list showing all subsequent citing sources.
3. Analyze the potential effect on the precedential weight of the cited case indicated by the analytical symbols provided by the citator. Consider limiting the list of citing sources by jurisdiction, headnote, date, or other function.
4. Prioritize and read the citing sources. Analyze the impact, if any, these sources have on the case being updated.

citator identifies later citing authority. Table 9-1 outlines the steps for updating online.

Before computerized citators were developed, updating was performed in print citators. By far the most comprehensive of print citators were the sets of *Shepard's Citations*, which were available for the published case law of the federal courts and all states, as well as some regulations, statutes, and law reviews. Many veteran attorneys still refer to updating, particularly of judicial decisions, as "Shepardizing." Shepard's online and KeyCite include a much broader range of authority than do the print *Shepard's* sets. The online versions are much more current and should always be preferred to print.[1]

II. Ethical Duty to Update

A lawyer is obligated to provide a client competent representation. "Competent representation requires the legal knowledge, skill, thoroughness and preparation reasonably necessary for the representa-

---

1. In situations where only print *Shepard's* are available, seek the help of a law librarian or consult the sample pages at the beginning of a *Shepard's* volume.

tion."[2] Determining the current status of the law is essential to competent representation. This determination can be a challenging and time-consuming part of the research process. It may be necessary to read many citing sources to determine what effect they may have on the meaning and weight of authority of a particular case. The same is true of updating other types of authority. Although updating is demanding and time-consuming, the researcher must not consider this to be merely a necessary but somewhat mechanical process. As citing sources are read, the researcher will not only determine whether a case is still "good law," but in the process will come to understand the case and the issues more thoroughly, and might even obtain valuable new insights.

III. Updating: Is a Case Still "Good Law"?

If a case is to be cited to a court as authority for a position, it is essential that it be "good law," or, if the authoritativeness of the case has been possibly diminished by later cases, that those later cases be disclosed to the court. Determining the treatment of a case by later citing cases is thus a main purpose of citators.

A. Shepard's on LexisNexis

Shepard's is a powerful tool, but also a complex one. In addition to the introduction supplied in this chapter, the researcher should use the LexisNexis "Help" feature and view the online tutorials.

1. Access the Citator

LexisNexis provides two ways to access the Shepard's citator. When the citation to a document is already known, the citation can be en-

---

2. Rule 1.1 Model Rules of Professional Conduct at www.americanbar. org/groups/professional_responsibility/publications/model_rules_of_ professional_conduct/rule_1_1_competence.html

tered directly into Shepard's. Click on the Shepard's tab at the top of the screen. A template in which the citation is to be entered appears. The "View Tutorial" link to the online tutorials is located just above the template. Viewing these tutorials the first time you use Shepard's will help you research more effectively. Citations must be entered in a format recognized by the citator. Click on "Citation Formats" to determine exactly how the document you are citing needs to be entered. Click on the "T" link and note the list of Texas materials that may be checked in Shepard's.

If a case has been located in LexisNexis and is on the screen, a Shepard's symbol appears in the upper bar just in front of the case name. The symbol indicates Shepard's evaluation of the effect of citing authorities on the validity of the cited case. A link saying "Shepardize" also appears in blue near the middle of the upper bar. Clicking on either the symbol or the Shepardize link opens a Shepard's report for the cited document.

2. Select Type of Cite List

The template accessed from the Shepard's tab has two radio buttons. To check to see whether a case or other document is still good law, click on "Shepard's for Validation." The other option, "Shepard's for Research," is discussed in Part IV. of this chapter. If you got a Shepard's report by linking from a document, clicking on "KWIC" in the upper, left-hand corner of the Shepard's report will give you the Shepard's for Validation report. Next to the KWIC link is one called "Full." The Full link produces the Shepard's for Research report.

3. Analyze Citator Symbols and Limit Search Results

At the top of the results page is a symbol representing Shepard's evaluation of the potential effect of citing cases on the precedential value of the cited case. See Table 9-2 for a selected list of Shepard's and KeyCite symbols and their meanings.

A red stop sign, for example, in Shepard's means the case has received negative treatment by later cases and may no longer be good

Table 9-2. Selected Symbols for Updating Cases
with KeyCite and Shepard's

KeyCite Symbol	Shepard's Symbol	Meaning
Red flag	Red stop sign	Negative treatment; the case may no longer be good law
Yellow flag	Yellow triangle	Possible negative treatment, though less strong than a red symbol
Green "C"	Green Diamond	Positive treatment
Blue "H"	Blue "A" or "I"	Citing sources are available

law. The meaning of each symbol can be revealed by hovering the cursor over the signal, and each Shepard's results page has a legend of all symbols at the bottom of the page. These symbols are useful, but they should not be given too much weight. Inexperienced researchers often immediately give up on cases with a red signal. Most cases include, and are cited for, more than one point of law. Negative treatment by a citing case might relate to a different issue in the cited case than the issue relevant to the research project. A later case may have overruled the case you are dealing with on one point, resulting in a red signal, while the case may still be good law for the point relevant to your research project. Also, your interpretation of the significance of a citing case's treatment of the cited case might differ from that of the LexisNexis editor who assigned the negative treatment tag. You must read the citing cases carefully and draw your own conclusions.

Figure 9-1 is a screen shot of the beginning of a Shepard's for Validation report for a case. At the top of the report, the title of the case and the parallel citations appear, along with the citator symbol and its meaning. Just below the case citation is the Shepard's summary, which appears in a gray box. The summary first states whether there is subsequent history and whether prior history is available. Prior history consists of the earlier decisions as the case moved through the litigation process. Subsequent history consists of later decisions concerning the case. Subsequent history decisions, when they exist, often affect the validity of the cited case, since they reverse, affirm, or otherwise decide the correctness of the cited case opinion upon appeal.

Figure 9-1. Shepard's for Validation Report

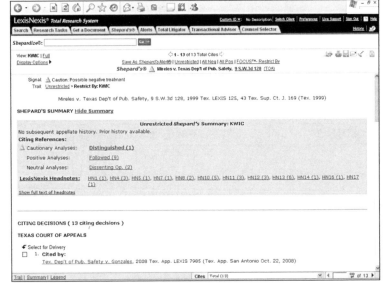

Source: LexisNexis. Copyright 2009 LexisNexis, a division of Reed Elsevier Inc. All Rights Reserved. LexisNexis and the Knowledge Burst are registered trademarks of Reed Elsevier Properties Inc. and are used with permission of LexisNexis.

To view the details of any prior or subsequent history, click on the link "Full" in the upper, right-hand corner.

Next is a summary of citing cases that may affect validity of the cited case. The citing cases in this report are classified as cautionary analyses, positive analyses, and neutral analyses. If a citing case over-ruled or questioned the cited case, a negative analysis would be indicated. The analyses summarized in the gray box only include the categories actually present in the report for the cited case. The number of cases of each type of analysis is in parentheses. Clicking on the link for a type of analysis, such as "Followed (9)," jumps to the first instance in the list. Clicking on the arrow in the lower, right-hand corner of the screen jumps to the next instance.

Next in the gray box is a heading, "LexisNexis Headnotes," followed by a listing of headnote (HN) numbers. The numbers in parentheses represent the count of the cases that Shepard's identifies as interpret-

Figure 9-2. Citing Cases in a Shepard's Report

Source: LexisNexis. Copyright 2009 LexisNexis, a division of Reed Elsevier Inc. All Rights Reserved. LexisNexis and the Knowledge Burst are registered trademarks of Reed Elsevier Properties Inc. and are used with permission of LexisNexis.

ing the point of law in the LexisNexis headnote with that number. When only cases interpreting the issue of a particular cited case headnote are wanted, this feature facilitates checking just those cases.

Under the gray box is a list of citing decisions. See Figure 9-2 for more of the report shown in Figure 9-1. Each citing case that may affect validity is identified by headers, such as "Distinguished by" or "Followed by." Reminder: if you were in the full Shepard's for Research display, clicking on KWIC would convert to the Shepard's for Validation display, limited to just these cases affecting validity.

The citing case information in Figure 9-2 includes pinpoint cites (cites to the exact page citing our case), LexisNexis headnote numbers, and a Shepard's symbol for the case. The Shepard's symbol is the symbol for that citing case and does not refer to the cited case for the report. Clicking on the citing case Shepard's symbol links to the Shepard's report for that citing case. The report can be customized to

Figure 9-3. Shepard's FOCUS Authority Limitation Template

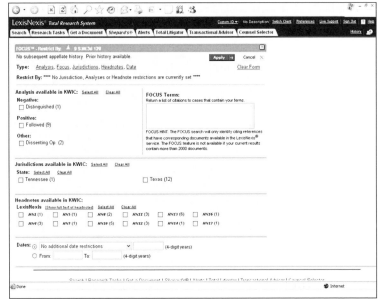

Source: LexisNexis. Copyright 2009 LexisNexis, a division of Reed Elsevier Inc. All Rights Reserved. LexisNexis and the Knowledge Burst are registered trademarks of Reed Elsevier Properties Inc. and are used with permission of LexisNexis.

display or not display the Shepard's symbols, pinpoint cites, and LexisNexis headnotes by selecting from the "Display Options" menu in the upper left-hand corner of the screen. Clicking on a highlighted case name opens a new window with the full text of the citing case.

Other options are available for customizing the report. In addition to the default unrestricted display, links at the middle top of the screen allow displaying all negative cites, all positive cites, or more elaborate limitations using "FOCUS — restrict by." Clicking on the FOCUS link opens a template allowing selection of citing authorities with certain characteristics. Figure 9-3 shows the authority limitation template.

The options presented in the template represent only the cites available in the particular Shepard's report. Particularly valuable is the ability to limit by headnote.

4. Limit by Headnote

Most cases address several points of law. LexisNexis, the West National Reporter System, and many state official reporters summarize these points of law in headnotes. (See Chapter 5 for a detailed discussion of headnotes.) A case might be reported in several print and online reporters, as well as in LexisNexis. The issues chosen for headnote treatment by the various reporters are not always the same, and the headnote numbers summarizing the same issue might not be the same in the different sources. FOCUS allows limiting the results to cases addressing the subject of the relevant LexisNexis headnote number in the cited case. Be sure to determine the LexisNexis headnote number in the cited case for the issue you are researching. The full text of the headnotes can be shown in the report by clicking on a link in the headnote area of the FOCUS template.

B. KeyCite on Westlaw

KeyCite is similar to Shepard's in many respects, but it has its own conventions and terminology. The researcher must understand the KeyCite conventions and terminology before beginning. Click on the KeyCite link at the top of the Westlaw screen for a detailed overview of the types of documents that can be checked on KeyCite, the coverage of citing references, the types of information provided about citing references, and explanations of the meaning of citator symbols as they are applied to different types of documents. From the overview page, there are links to a list of publications included in KeyCite, tips for use, and information about the KeyCite Alert service.

Like Shepard's, KeyCite allows for updating cases, statutes, regulations, patents, and other types of authority. The following discussion deals specifically with case updating.

1. Access the Citator

KeyCite can be accessed from several points: from the KeyCite link at the top of the screen; by clicking on the KeyCite citator symbol, such as a red flag, near the top of a document; by entering a cite in

Figure 9-4. Full History on KeyCite

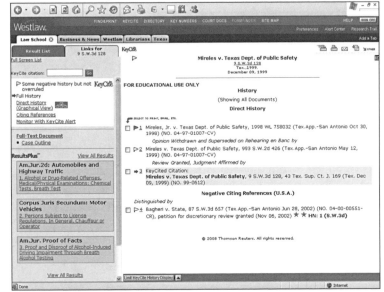

Source: Westlaw. Reprinted with permission of Thomson Reuters.

the KeyCite search box in the left frame; or by clicking on links to KeyCite wherever they appear.

2. Select Type of Cite List

Once a KeyCite search has been entered, or a report has been linked to, a report will appear. The right frame of the screen contains the report, while the left frame provides, along with other features, several options for the display and a brief explanation of the meaning of the citator symbol for the case. See Figure 9-4 for a screenshot of a Full History on KeyCite.

The default display is "Full History." The KeyCite Full History display is similar to the Shepard's for Validation display. Both focus on the citing references the services consider most relevant to whether the cited case is still "good law." Notice, however, that KeyCite's Full History displays the prior history cases, which were only referred to in the Shepard's for Validation report. The cited case is highlighted by a gray bar. If there were subsequent history cases, they would appear after the cited cases. Since the relation among the cases in the direct history can be complex, KeyCite provides a Direct History "Graphical View" option. Clicking on the link in the left frame opens a screen with the relation between the cases in the direct history depicted graphically. The "Negative References" in a report are cases considered by Westlaw to reduce the precedential value of the cited case.

Note that, unlike the Shepard's for Validation report, the KeyCite Full History report does not include the cases that followed the case being updated or cases that cite it in a dissenting opinion. These do appear, however, in the citing references list. If the link "Citing References" in the left frame is selected, the display will change to include all citing references. This option, useful for using KeyCite to extend case research, is discussed later in this chapter.

3. Analyze Citator Symbols and Limit Search Results

At the top of the KeyCite display screen is a citator symbol. The meaning of KeyCite symbols is summarized in Table 9-2 and online at the Westlaw KeyCite overview. As with Shepard's symbols, KeyCite symbols are useful indicators, but must not be given too much weight. Negative treatment by a citing case might relate to a different issue in the cited case from the issue relevant to the research project. It might also happen that your interpretation of the significance of a citing case's treatment of the cited case differs from that of the Westlaw editor who assigned the negative treatment symbol. It is always necessary to read the citing cases carefully and draw your own conclusions.

Citator symbols also appear to the left of each citing case in the KeyCite report. The symbols indicate the KeyCite evaluation of the validity of citing cases. Clicking on the symbol next to a citing case opens the KeyCite report for that case. Although these symbols do not relate directly to the cited case, if a citing case is itself evaluated as having low validity, its treatment of the cited case might be less significant. Again, this cannot be assumed. A negative citing case with a cautionary symbol must be read carefully and the reasons for the cautionary signal evaluated to see if they bear any relation to the relevant issues in the cited case. The issues in the cited case that are discussed by the citing cases are identified by the headnote numbers at the end of the citing case notation.

As with Shepard's, the report can be limited to only show cases and other citing documents with certain characteristics. Click on the "Limit KeyCite Display" button in the bottom-left corner of the right frame. A template appears in which to select limitations by document type, headnote, words found by Westlaw's "Locate" feature, jurisdiction, date, and depth of treatment.

4. Limiting by Headnote

Limiting by headnote number can be very useful in restricting to only those cases addressing the issue in the cited case relevant to your research. KeyCite's headnote limitation only applies to West reporter headnotes. The headnote limitation in KeyCite is actually a search in the West topic and key number system, and thus similar to a West digest search (described in Chapter 5).

C. Texas Subsequent History in Shepard's and KeyCite

The detailed subsequent history notations for cases appealed from a Texas court of appeals to the Texas Supreme Court or the Texas Court of Criminal Appeals were discussed in Chapter 4. (See Appendix A for further information on proper citation.) Shepard's and KeyCite do generally supply headers telling how a petition for review or writ of error from a Texas court of appeals decision was treated by the higher court. The *Greenbook*, however, advises in a practice tip: "Petition status and history is often available electronically through Lexis or Westlaw. However, it is best to consult West's *Texas Subsequent History Table*, which is supplemented in the advance sheets of the *South Western Reporter (Texas Cases)*."[3]

IV. Using Citators as Case-Finding Tools

Earlier chapters discussed finding cases using annotated codes and constitutions, digests, and online search techniques. Research using

---

3. Texas Law Review Ass'n, *The Greenbook: Texas Rules of Form* 21, 24 (12th ed. 2010).

some combination of these approaches will usually produce relevant cases. The researcher will use a citator to check whether the cases found are good law. The citator can also be used to see if additional relevant cases are available, as well as identifying other useful citing authority.

A. Extending Case Research

Shepard's and KeyCite both have options for viewing all citing references, not just references considered by their editors to affect the validity of the cited case. In Shepard's, select "Shepard's for Research" when entering a citation, or, if already viewing a Shepard's report, click on "Full." All citing references will appear, with cases first, followed by secondary authority. As mentioned above, the citing references can be limited to specific jurisdictions or by other characteristics. The citing cases are ordered with decisions by the highest court at the top of the list, followed by successively lower courts.

In KeyCite, click on "Citing References" in the left frame. All citing cases will appear. The list of citing cases is followed by citing secondary authority and court documents. KeyCite ranks the cases using signals indicating depth of treatment by the citing cases, with four stars indicating extensive analysis, three stars indicating substantial analysis, two stars indicating some discussion, and one star for a mere mention, as in a string cite. KeyCite also puts quotation marks by citing cases that have quoted the cited case.

Examine the citing cases to see if any cases appear that were not found in previous stages of the research project. The citing cases deal in some way with the issues in the cases you have found, and thus may supply valuable additions to your analysis. Be sure to check the headnote numbers as a quick guide to the relevance of the citing cases to your issues. Importantly, the cases found using the citator are likely to comprise a link in a chain of case authority leading to the current state of case law and may also clarify the relation of relevant cases to each other.

Following the citing cases are citing references to other types of authority, such as law review articles, A.L.R. annotations, and court documents. Commentary that cites a case may contain useful insights into the research issue. Remember that the research process is iterative. Even though you began the research project in secondary authority and then moved on to searching primary authority, do not hesitate to pursue possibly useful commentary discovered later in the process.

The citator can also be used to extend the chain of case authority back in time. Shepard's and KeyCite both provide table of authority services, accessed by clicking on a "TOA" link. The Shepard's TOA link appears at the top of the report, right after the case citation, while KeyCite's link is near the bottom of the left frame. The table of authorities is a list of the cases cited by the case you are checking in the citator. The table of authorities helps the researcher understand the full chain of case authority, extending from the past, through the cited case, and up to the present time. Of course, the table of authorities can also be determined by reading a case and noting the cases cited by that case. The TOA feature allows for a quick summarization and supplies the citator symbols and access to the citator report for each of the cases, as well as quick access to the text of each case.

B. Finding Cases Interpreting Statutes and Regulations

As discussed in Chapters 6 and 8, it is necessary to find judicial decisions interpreting statutes and to find administrative agency decisions and judicial decisions interpreting agency rules. Shepard's and KeyCite can be used to find cases interpreting statutes and regulations. Both allow updating of the *United States Code* and *Code of Federal Regulations* cites. All state codes are included, but regulatory code coverage is less complete and should be checked for the state being researched. For Texas, statutes and the administrative code can be checked in Shepard's and KeyCite.

The non-citator tools for finding cases interpreting statutes are very good. Annotated codes, whether in print or online, include the cases interpreting federal and state statutes, and keyword searches and digest topic and key number searches can be used as back-ups. Searches in Shepard's and KeyCite, however, have the advantage of supplying the Shepard's or KeyCite symbol and analysis for citing cases, and may sometimes turn up cases not found using the traditional finding tools.

In contrast, the ability to search for citing references to rules and regulations is a significant contribution to legal research. Except for a small number of titles, the *Code of Federal Regulations* does not come in an annotated version, and structuring keyword searches to capture all references to regulations is tricky. Finding cases and, particularly, agency decisions for state agency rules is even more challenging. The researcher should check Shepard's and KeyCite for citing references to any federal or state regulation being researched. Once agency decisions are identified as citing references, the text will be available from the citing reference note. This is a valuable feature, since the texts of agency decisions have often been difficult to locate. Remember to check the scope of Shepard's and KeyCite to see which agency decisions are available through each service.

V. Reading, Analyzing, and Updating Cases Found

Throughout the research process, as you find cases they should be checked in Shepard's or KeyCite to see how their precedential value has been affected by later opinions. When searching or reading cases in LexisNexis or Westlaw, look for the citator symbols at the top of the screen. Be careful to note the cases identified as overruling or otherwise reducing a case's validity. These may be key cases for the analysis and, if favoring the other side in a dispute, are very likely to be relied upon by opposing counsel. Remember also that it is the duty of counsel to disclose to the court case law that does not support the client's position. Updating to determine if cases and other authorities are good law must be performed as the last step before submitting your research document. The new case, statute, or regulation affecting your issue may have appeared just yesterday.

It is best to read all citing cases. Some cases have, however, been cited by hundreds or thousands of other cases. In such instances, some citing references are important, while many add little or nothing to the state of the law. Limiting citator searches, especially by jurisdiction and headnote, can help greatly by reducing the number of citing references that must be perused and considered for further reading. When faced with more cases than can be read within the scope of the project, prioritize the cases to be read by these criteria:

- Focus on negative treatments first. Read any case that reverses, overrides, criticizes, or distinguishes your case.
- Read cases from your jurisdiction first. Cases from other jurisdictions are persuasive authority only.
- Read cases from the highest courts first. Next, read cases from the intermediate appellate courts. If the opinions of trial courts are published in your jurisdiction (Texas trial courts do not publish opinions), these are the least persuasive.
- Read more recent cases first. Careful reading of recent cases often indicates which older cases may or may not deserve your attention.
- Read the cases cited for the headnotes for the issues relevant to your research.

As you find cases and pursue citing references, you will see trends and lines of authority leading to the current state of the case law. Concentrate on the frequently cited and clearly influential cases in forming your arguments. Use little-cited cases or cases from other jurisdictions only as a last resort or, perhaps, to add weight to an already well-supported analysis.

VI. Other Online Updating Tools

During the course of a research project, it is important to learn of new cases, statutes, or regulations that may change the law or affect the validity of authorities already found. Shepard's and KeyCite allow saving a citator search as an alert. The Shepard's alert or KeyCite alert transmits email notices of new citing references as they are entered into LexisNexis or Westlaw. Many state governments also provide alerts of new developments. In Texas, the state legislature's website allows subscribers to set alerts for new developments in the legislature.[4] Automated alerts can also be set for Texas state agency rule making.[5] The federal regulations.gov site[6] provides an alert service for new rule-making notices in the *Federal Register*. West's "Agency Tracker" alert service allows automated tracking and notification of federal agency postings in the *Federal Register*.

Westlaw and LexisNexis also allow alerts to be set for new information appearing in almost any database. Westlaw's "Alert Center" and LexisNexis' "Alerts" services run a search query in designated databases at intervals set by the user. Delivery of alerts is by email or transmission directly to printer or fax machine. Particularly in projects where important information may appear in general or specialized news sources, these alerts are very useful.

---

4. The address is www.legis.state.tx.us/Home.aspx.
5. The secretary of state's website provides this feature at www.sos.state.tx.us/texreg/subinfo.shtml.
6. The address is www.regulations.gov/#home.

Chapter 10

Secondary Sources

I. Not "Secondary" in the Research Process

Previous chapters have explored the types of primary legal authority, the statements of the law produced by persons or bodies acting with authority of the government. Although the legal researcher must locate the relevant primary authority, searching in the resources containing primary authority is often not the best way to begin a research project. In fact, when searching in complex or unfamiliar areas of the law, beginning with searches in primary authority might lead to disastrous results. The researcher should begin many projects in secondary sources; in the research process, they are not "secondary" at all, but tools of prime importance.

Anybody beginning a study of any area of the law soon realizes it is vast and complex. Lawyers, judges, and legal scholars have invested great time and effort to master it. Some of these experts write commentary, syntheses of the primary authorities that pull together the law from the primary authorities and explain it in a manner understandable by the newcomer to the area. You should take advantage of this work by others, rather than reinvent the wheel. Starting in secondary authority will you give an overview of the current status of the law in an area and its history. It will introduce the researcher to the essential concepts and the terminology needed to formulate search terms and to understand what you find. Secondary authority also contains citations to key statutes, regulations, and cases. These citations often provide excellent places to begin research in the primary authority.

This chapter discusses legal encyclopedias, legal periodicals, treatises, practice oriented materials, *American Law Reports* (A.L.R.),

Table 10-1. Outline for Researching Secondary Sources

1. Generate a list of search terms.
2. Search the library's catalog for the location of secondary sources.
3. Search the index of a secondary source.
4. Find the relevant portion of the main volumes. Read the commentary to gain understanding of the legal issues. If primary authority is cited, record the cites in your journal for later reference.
5. Update the secondary source, if possible.
6. Read primary authority.

"mini-libraries," the restatements of the law, uniform law and model codes, and resources for researching issues in professional ethics. Some of the resources, such as A.L.R. and mini-libraries, contain primary law in addition to secondary resources. They are included in this chapter because their primary role is to introduce, explain, and assist with research on complex, specialized legal topics.

See Table 10-1 for a summary of the steps involved in using secondary sources. You should give careful consideration to whether to use secondary sources in print or online format, rather than assume the online version will be best for any purpose. While online resources are often very useful for locating secondary sources or for a quick perusal of documents, many researchers find that scanning of the text for relevant portions and the sustained, close reading of those found is often done most effectively in print.

II. Legal Encyclopedias

A. General Comments

Legal encyclopedias attempt to encompass the entire body of law in a jurisdiction. For each topic within that body of law, they provide brief summaries of the law of that topic. They may identify conflicts or differences between lines of authority, but they do not provide deep analysis or policy discussions. Since they attempt to summarize the law into brief "black letter" rules, much of the subtlety and underlying uncertainty of the law is lost. For this reason, the researcher may choose to begin research in an encyclopedia, but will move on to the more sophisticated commentary provided by some of the other resources discussed in this chapter. Do not cite encyclopedias as authority.

B. *Texas Jurisprudence, 3d*

Texas Jurisprudence, 3d[1] is a West encyclopedia specifically for Texas law. This is the current edition of the *Texas Jurisprudence* encyclopedias and is kept up to date by pocket parts and replacement volumes. Since its focus is on Texas law, it will be more pertinent on many issues than are the national encyclopedias, discussed below.

Look for relevant materials in the print versions by using the index or the table of contents. It is usually most efficient to start by looking in the index volumes, located at the end of the set, using the search terms prepared in the early stages of the research process. The index entries indicate a topic, called an "article" in *Texas Jurisprudence, 3d*, and section number within that topic. The name of the topic is often abbreviated; a table at the beginning of each volume gives the full name of the topic for each abbreviation. If the search of the index is unsuccessful, the next step is to look through the table of contents. Often, the topic containing the issue is evident.

The next step is to go to the volume in which that topic begins and look through the detailed table of contents for relevant sections. The text of the sections summarizes the law and cites supporting authority. The footnotes also contain references to particular forms in form books (discussed below) and to A.L.R. annotations (discussed below).

---

1. This is the full title. Confusingly, the books show the title as *Texas Jur III*. In most library catalogs, a title search on either *Texas Jur* or *Texas Jurisprudence* will find the record.

The cases in the footnotes might be only selected, representative cases on the point and might be quite dated. Although it is necessary to do further research for cases, using the techniques explained in Chapter 5, the cases cited in the encyclopedia should be good starting places for case research, using key number searching and citators to expand the search for cases. References to statutes and rules tend to be spotty; search for statutes and rules thoroughly using the techniques explained in Chapters 6 and 8. As with any other supplemented work, you must check the pocket parts for updates to the text and footnote citations.

Texas Jurisprudence, 3d also supplies references to other research resources, such as A.L.R. annotations, practice guides and form books, and key numbers for research in the digests. The set also contains a set of Words and Phrases volumes, containing headnotes to the Texas cases from the comprehensive *Words and Phrases*. *Texas Jurisprudence, 3d* is also found on Westlaw, where it may be searched using the table of contents or with full-text searching techniques.

C. National Legal Encyclopedias

The major encyclopedias covering the whole of American law are *Corpus Juris Secundum* (C.J.S.) and *American Jurisprudence, Second Edition* (Am. Jur. 2d). Although both are now published by West, they differ somewhat in emphasis and coverage. Since they are national in scope, they must give general statements for law that may differ greatly between jurisdictions. They are most useful for federal law research and overviews of fairly standardized areas of the law. For research specifically on matters of Texas law, use *Texas Jurisprudence, 3d*.

The national encyclopedias are searched with the same techniques described for *Texas Jurisprudence, 3d*. Additional useful features found in C.J.S. and Am. Jur. 2d are annual supplemental volumes containing tables showing where to find discussions of sections of the U.S.C. and C.F.R., public laws and major acts, federal rules of civil and criminal procedure, and other commonly used authorities. Both encyclopedias are found on Westlaw, while Am. Jur. 2d is only on LexisNexis. They may be searched using the tables of contents or with full-text searching techniques.

III. Legal Periodicals

A. Law Reviews and Law Journals

Law reviews and law journals publish scholarly articles by law professors, law students, lawyers, and judges. The articles delve deeply into narrow topics. They typically present a thoroughly researched summary of the current state of the law on some issue, then develop a new perspective or propose a policy, rule, or practice the author considers an improvement on the existing law. The survey of the current state of the law can be very useful. The policy analyses and proposals for new approaches may help develop new perspectives and arguments, and they may provide alternatives to the existing law for the lawyer hoping to persuade a judge, administrative agency, or legislature to consider changes to the existing law.

The typical issue of a law review or law journal includes several leading articles, usually written by law professors, one or more lengthy book reviews, and student-written "Notes" or "Comments," or the briefer "Case Notes." Student-written contributions do not carry the authority of the articles by established experts, but they are usually well-researched and well-written.

Most law reviews and law journals are produced and edited by law students chosen either for high grades or through writing competitions at the end of their first year of law school. The term "law review" tends to be used for the more prestigious flagship publication of a law school, which typically publishes articles on diverse legal topics for a broad audience. The term "law journal" more often refers to other scholarly publications of a law school, often with a specialized focus, such as the *Houston Journal of International Law* or the *Texas Journal of Oil, Gas, and Energy Law*. Prominent exceptions to this general rule exist, such as the very prestigious *Yale Law Journal*, the flagship publication for Yale Law School. A few law journals are "peer-reviewed," meaning that law professors review, select, and comment on or suggest changes to submitted articles. The *Journal of Legal Education* and *Legal Writing: The Journal of the Legal Writing Institute* are well-known, peer-reviewed journals.

Law reviews and law journals typically appear several times a year in paperback issues. Law libraries often gather together the issues for a year and bind them into a hardbound volume for preservation and ease of shelving. Once published, articles are not updated. Most articles are read and cited most in the first few years after publication. A measure of the influence of an article is how often it is cited by other articles. This can be determined by searching the Westlaw or LexisNexis legal periodical databases or KeyCite or Shepard's for references to the article. The influence of legal scholars and the prestige of schools are often measured by citation studies, as well.

B. Bar Journals

The American Bar Association (A.B.A.), state bar associations, and some local bar associations publish journals. Bar journals commonly contain articles written by practicing lawyers and judges, and tend to focus on recent developments in legal practice, the law of the jurisdiction, or a specialized topic served by the journal. Although not as scholarly as the articles in law reviews or law journals, the articles are generally well-researched, thoughtful, and well-written. They are unlikely to be cited in leading academic journals, but can be extremely useful. Bar journals also provide valuable information about lawyers and judges, legal news, changes in court rules, disciplinary proceedings, and recent court decisions or legislation. The journal for the State Bar of Texas is the *Texas Bar Journal*. As in many states, the current issue of the *Texas Bar Journal* and archives of previous issues are available at the webpage of the State Bar of Texas.[2]

---

2. The address is www.texasbar.com. Click on "News and Publications," and then on "Texas Bar Journal."

C. How to Find Articles

For relatively recent articles,[3] Westlaw and LexisNexis databases of legal periodicals can be searched using the full-text searching methods described in Chapter 2. A focused search in the title field or segment is often the most efficient.

Since Westlaw and LexisNexis do not cover all journals and their time coverage is limited, specialized indexes for legal periodicals often yield more complete results. A database called LegalTrac, available in many law libraries, has coverage from 1981 for almost all law reviews and law journals, bar journals, and other legal periodicals. Although it contains some full-text copies of articles, most items found will be brief records of articles, often with an abstract of the article, and the citation to the article. The researcher uses the citation to locate the text of the article. LegalTrac is the online version of an index known in print as the *Current Law Index* and on Westlaw and LexisNexis as the Legal Resources Index (L.R.I.).

An alternative index is the *Index to Legal Periodicals and Books* (I.L.P.B.), formerly the *Index to Legal Periodicals*. The I.L.P.B. is particularly valuable when older articles are being sought; it has been indexing articles continuously since 1926. Most academic law libraries have a complete set of the I.L.P.B. It is also available in online format; the researcher might find it included in a Westlaw subscription.

Another resource for finding legal periodical articles is HeinOnline. Although designed primarily to supply images of law review and law journal articles, it also has search capacities, although less sophisticated than those on Westlaw or LexisNexis. HeinOnline is subscribed to by most academic law libraries and by some law firm libraries.

Also worthy of note are online repositories LSN/SSRN[4] and Be-Press.[5] These websites allow authors to post articles online for down-

---

3. The coverage for most journals in Westlaw and LexisNexis starts in the 1980s.
4. The address is www.ssrn.com/lsn/index.html.
5. The address is http://law.bepress.com/repository.

loading by others. Legal scholars can post on these sites both their published articles and their forthcoming articles or works in progress. They are becoming very popular as scholars attempt to maximize the availability of their work to both professional and lay audiences.

IV. Treatises, Hornbooks, and Nutshells

Treatises are works of commentary on a legal topic, such as torts, bankruptcy, or securities law. They are written by legal scholars who are recognized experts on the topic and focus on providing a comprehensive view of the law, including exploring divisions of authority and suggesting the better rule or policy. The term "treatise" tends to be reserved for the extensive commentaries on a topic, with more compact works being called "hornbooks" or "nutshells." The hornbook and nutshell on a topic might be written by the author of a major treatise on the same topic. Hornbooks are sometimes abridgements of a major treatise, making pursuing further reading in the treatise more convenient. While hornbooks are often viewed as study aids, they can also be useful for initial background reading in a topic. Hornbooks are more detailed and analytical than nutshells and have more extensive footnotes and research references. Nutshells, published in the United States by West, are very brief and best used as study aids by students reviewing a course or by the person seeking only a quick refresher on a basic point of law.

Most treatises are updated regularly, either by pocket parts or supplemental volumes (for treatises published in book format), or by replacement pages or supplemental sections (for treatises issued in three-ring binders). A hornbook might be supplemented by pocket parts, but hornbooks and nutshells are commonly updated by publication of new editions of a title.

Many researchers prefer to read these works in print format. Also, not all treatises are available online. To locate a treatise, hornbook, or nutshell in a library, use the library's online catalog. If the author's name is known, it can be searched for in the author field, often found under the "Advanced" search options. If books on a particular topic are sought, a search in the title field using just the word for the topic, such as "torts" or "contracts," is most effective. If too many titles appear in the results, try adding "treatise" or a similar term to the query. Once one book on the subject has been found in the catalog, others can be found by clicking on the subject identifiers near the bottom of the record.

Since books in libraries are organized according to subject, it also pays to search the books immediately on either side of the book found. This can be done in most online catalogs by clicking on the highlighted "call number." An example of a call number is KF170.A6 2d, the unique number indicating the location of *American Jurisprudence Legal Forms* in the library. The titles on either side of the book can be browsed online. It is often even more effective to go the shelf where the book is and investigate the books in that area.

Many treatises are found in Westlaw and LexisNexis. If Westlaw or LexisNexis has a "library" of resources relating to the topic being researched, try looking there for the secondary sources. If not, use the directory to locate likely resources. Not all treatises are found in Westlaw or LexisNexis. Law libraries subscribe to a number of databases, such as the C.C.H. and B.N.A. collections of databases, to supplement the contents of Westlaw and LexisNexis. These should also be explored for treatises. Be aware that not all treatises are available online.

V. Practitioner-Oriented Materials

Practitioners often need quick and efficient guides to how to perform the many tasks required in the practice of law, such as complying with the rules and procedures of local courts, drafting court documents and transactional documents, preparing for trial, and just keeping up with the many developments in the law. A number of practitioner-oriented publications meet these needs.

A. Practice and Procedure Guides

The Texas practitioner has many publications available concerning the practice of law in many specialized areas. Often, such books have titles including the phrases "law and practice," "handbook," "guide," or "practice and procedure," denoting their "how to do it" orientation. Prominent examples are *Dorsaneo, Texas Litigation Guide,* and the multi-volume *Texas Practice* set. Such books often contain discussion of the essentials of the law on the topic but with a more practical focus than the scholarly approach typical of treatises. Practice and procedure guides can be found in the library catalog using the techniques discussed above for finding treatises. The lawyer preparing for trial should also be aware of three national publications giving very detailed background discussion, instructions, forms, and research references for preparing and conducting trials on specific issues. These publications are *Am. Jur. Trials, Causes of Action,* and *Proof of Facts.*

B. Forms and Form Books

Lawyers have always used documents produced previously by themselves or others as an aid to drafting new documents. These may be in the firm's own files or found in such books as the practice guides just discussed. There are also books devoted to "forms," representative samples of documents for transactions or for court proceedings. An example of a transactional document would be a contract for the sale of land. Examples of court documents would be a complaint or reply. Form books may be encyclopedic, attempting to provide forms for almost all purposes. Examples of encyclopedic form books are *West's Texas Forms,* or, at the national level, *American Jurisprudence Pleading and Practice Forms* and *American Jurisprudence Legal Forms.*

Legal forms are *not* "fill in the blanks" forms. It is essential to thoroughly research and understand the law relative to the form and the meaning and purpose of everything in the document to be drafted. For this reason, the better form books contain not just sample documents, but also discussion of the relevant law, references to other research resources, checklists of information to be gathered and factors to be considered, suggested alternative clauses, and other aids to drafting. A form in a form book might be poorly drafted and require extensive rewriting. The good drafter will concentrate not just on the law and lists of contents, but also on clear organization and precise expression. Many books are available on how to draft clearly written and well-organized documents.

Many of the popular form books are also available on Westlaw and LexisNexis. Free online forms are found at a number of sites on the Internet. Online form sites generally do not provide significant research support and the forms are often of uncertain origin; they must be used with great caution. Required forms are sometimes included in statutory or regulatory codes. Examples are required quitclaim deed and power of attorney forms in many state codes and the mandatory bankruptcy forms in the United States Code. Useful forms are sometimes also found in collections of court rules, in practice guides and handbooks, in continuing legal education materials, and in some treatises. A keyword search on "form" or "forms" in an online library catalog will often reveal the presence of these.

C. Continuing Legal Education Materials

The State Bar of Texas, like many state bars, requires all members to take continuing legal education (C.L.E.) instruction. The state bar, law schools, and other organizations organize courses approved for C.L.E. credits. These courses may be prepared and presented by practitioners, judges, law professors, or other professionals, and deal with specialized topics, often focusing on recent developments in the law or practice in the jurisdiction. The materials prepared for the courses are often published and sold separately from the course. Law libraries often collect these publications. C.L.E. courses and similar publications are also prepared at the national level, with prominent publishers being the Practising Law Institute (P.L.I.), American Law Institute (A.L.I.), and the A.B.A.

C.L.E. materials tend to deal with cutting-edge developments and many are not updated until the course is repeated. Be sure to check the date of the materials to be sure they are not outdated.

VI. *American Law Reports* (A.L.R.)

American Law Reports (A.L.R.) is a unique resource. Published since 1919, the A.L.R. is now in its sixth series, and the related *A.L.R. Federal* is now in its second series. Although the A.L.R. series contain some primary authority, they are primarily secondary sources in that their function is to assist the researcher in finding and understanding the primary law regarding an issue.

The substance of the A.L.R. series is in the "annotations." Each annotation explores in detail a legal issue that was the subject of a recently reported case. That case is printed in the same volume as the annotation, but the case is also printed in one of the West reporters. The annotation, written by a West editor, presents the results of thorough research in a narrow area. For example, the annotation found in 33 A.L.R. 6th 1 has as its subject "Basis for Exclusion of Public from State Criminal Trial in Order to Preserve Safety, Confidentiality, or Well-Being of Witness Who Is Not Undercover Police Officer."

The annotation defines the issue, provides citations to other secondary sources relating to the issue, and includes a "Table of Cases, Laws, and Rules," which cites cases from the federal and state courts and the statutes, rules, regulations, and constitutional provisions bearing on the subject found in those cases. The annotation attempts to be comprehensive in its coverage of case law, but the coverage of non-case law primary authority may be less complete. Following these preliminary materials, the annotation focuses on summaries of the cases and the interpretation they support. The annotation is thus a useful collection and elucidation of the case law regarding a narrow issue, but does not provide commentary at the level of sophistication found in treatises.

In order to locate A.L.R. annotations, start with the *A.L.R. Quick Index* or the *A.L.R. Federal Quick Index*, depending on whether the issue is primarily one of state or federal law. If nothing is found in the quick indexes, the more comprehensive *A.L.R. Index*, covering the second through sixth A.L.R. series and the first and second series of the *A.L.R. Federal*, should be searched. Look for the most recent annotation listed for the issue. After locating a cite to an annotation, check the "Annotation History Table" to see if the annotation has been superseded or supplemented by a more recent annotation. When using any annotation, be sure to update using the pocket parts.

A.L.R. annotations are also found in Westlaw, in the "Secondary Resources" directory. LexisNexis no longer carries the A.L.R.

VII. Looseleaf Services: The "Mini-Libraries"

A. Print Versions

Looseleaf services, sometimes referred to as "mini-libraries," are very useful tools for finding and using primary authority relating to a particular topic. They are included in this chapter because their primary purpose is to pull together the primary law for researchers in that topic, make access to the law available with good finding tools and organization, and provide commentary to explain the law. The best-known publishers of these services are C.C.H., B.N.A., and R.I.A. Many looseleaf services deal with specialized practice areas, often heavily regulated, in which the law changes rapidly and the practitioner does most research in a circumscribed body of statutory, regulatory, and case law. Examples of such areas are tax and labor law.

Looseleaf services are published in three-ring binders holding separate pages. The publishers update the contents of the service by sending packages of updated pages, together with instructions telling what pages to discard and where to place the new pages.[6] The services can thus be kept very current, as pages are updated as often as sev-

---

6. Not every legal publication in a three-ring binder is a looseleaf service. Some works are published in ring binders for convenience, but may be updated infrequently or with supplements simply added behind the material already in the binder.

eral times a month. The typical looseleaf service contains statutes and code sections, regulations of administrative agencies, abstracts of cases, and practitioner-oriented discussion of the law. A very important function long provided by some services was gathering and making available the judicial decisions of administrative agencies. The only reporters for the decisions of many agencies were extensions of the looseleaf services in an era when those decisions were difficult to obtain. Although recent agency decisions are much more available in the Internet era, those reporters remain important for access to agency decisions, particularly older decisions.

Looseleaf services can be complex, and their organization varies greatly from one to the next. Start research in an unfamiliar service by reading the "How to Use" section. If you are not already familiar with the topic, start in the topical index or the table of contents. Case research is often supported by a digest of case abstracts, often citing to the reporter set affiliated with the service. The researcher with some knowledge of the topic can often go directly to the relevant portion of the service. The *CCH Standard Federal Tax Reporter*, for example, is organized by Internal Revenue Code section number. One feature that often confuses the new user is that pages have both page numbers and paragraph numbers. The paragraph numbers allow permanent reference points when pages are continually being removed and added; the location numbers found in the topical index will be to the paragraph numbers.

B. Online Versions

Although developed as print research tools, many mini-libraries are now available as online databases. Many law libraries subscribe to the online databases of C.C.H., B.N.A., and R.I.A. for access to critical resources not found on Westlaw or LexisNexis. Check your law library web page or ask a librarian about the availability of these resources. Some of the online versions are quite similar in organization and appearance to the print originals, while some are quite different. The vendors also change them, sometimes dramatically, in order to make them more usable.

Just as the "How to Use" section is the place to start in a print looseleaf service, the first step in using the online version should be using the tutorials or guides to the database. If the mini-library is available in both online and print versions, compare the usability of each. It is common for a researcher to prefer the online version of one mini-library, while finding the print looseleaf version of another more usable.

If a library has a collection of B.N.A. online materials, the researcher should also see which of the many very useful B.N.A. topical newsletters are available. These newsletters are very popular with subject specialists, and the online versions allow subscribers to set up email notifications of news on the topic.

VIII. Restatements

In the early twentieth century the American Law Institute (A.L.I.) undertook to identify and state the rules of law developed by the courts in subjects of the common law. Examples are the *Restatement of Torts* and *Restatement of Contracts*. The project has continued to the present, with many restatements now being in their second or third editions and new restatements being added.

Each restatement is prepared by a committee of lawyers, judges, and legal scholars, led by a "reporter." The committee analyzes the cases and derives a rule meant to state clearly and concisely the rule the courts have applied in reaching their decisions. The cases may not agree on the rule; the early restatements generally stated the most commonly applied rule, but in later restatements the rule stated is sometimes the rule the reporter and committee consider the better rule, or what they believe the rule should be. The "black letter" rules of the restatements are given numbers and stated much as a statutory rule would be stated. The Comments & Illustrations and Reporter's Notes following each rule provide summaries of cases to show the origin of the rule and examples of its application, as well as discussion by the reporter.

The restatements, as syntheses of case law, are secondary authority. Courts do, however, sometimes announce that they adopt a restatement rule as the rule of the jurisdiction. If so, the rule, commentary, and notes may be useful for understanding the law of the jurisdiction. Even then, though, be sure to study carefully the opinions from the courts of the jurisdiction in order to understand how the courts actually apply the rule to particular facts.

Restatements can be found in the library by searching the catalog for the subject of the restatement. For example, a title word search on "contracts" and "restatement" should yield the record for the editions of the *Restatement of Contracts*. Some libraries shelve all the restatements together, rather than separately with other works on the same subject. A librarian can direct you to that location. To find a rule in a restatement, use the index or the table of contents. The restatements can be found in Westlaw in the Secondary Resources directory and in LexisNexis in the Secondary Legal directory.

Restatements are not revised until a new edition is issued, but appendix volumes and pocket parts supply abstracts and citations to later cases citing the restatement. The set of volumes of a restatement can be somewhat confusing to the first-time user. Spend a little time examining the descriptions on the spines of the books and their contents before beginning to use a set.

IX. Uniform Laws and Model Codes

"Uniform laws" and "model codes" have been developed for many areas of the law by organizations hoping to bring uniformity to the laws of the states and to propose the best rules for general adoption. For example, much commercial law was once largely a matter of common law. It was highly fragmented and the terminology and rules varied greatly by state. The *Uniform Commercial Code* (U.C.C.) was developed to create a uniform body of commercial law in the United States. The U.C.C. has been adopted by all fifty states, although the states often change the language of some sections or choose different options in the U.C.C. when they enact it into legislation. Once a uniform code or model law is adopted in a state, the enacted language is the primary law in the state, and the research in it would be conducted using the techniques discussed in earlier chapters. The commentary and notes to the uniform law or model code may be useful secondary sources and, together with cases from other adopting states, may be valuable persuasive authority.

The most prominent of the organizations developing uniform laws is the National Conference of Commissioners on Uniform State Law (N.C.C.U.S.L.). The work is done by lawyers, judges, and legal scholars selected for expertise in the subject of a proposed uniform law. They produce drafts, distribute them for comments, and produce the final draft. After approval by the organization, the text of the uniform law and its comments and notes are published by N.C.C.U.S.L. Commercial publishers also publish uniform laws approved by N.C.C.U.S.L. West publishes uniform laws in *Uniform Laws Annotated* (U.L.A.), which supplements the text and comments from N.C.C.U.S.L. with indexes, research references, and tables showing the states that have adopted the laws and the dates of adoption. The U.L.A. also includes West headnotes from cases that have interpreted uniform laws adopted by states.

Uniform laws and model codes can be found in a library's online catalog with title word searches, such as "uniform law" or "model code." Browsing the shelves in the area of the stacks holding a subject area can also be useful, especially for comparing various resources containing the uniform laws or model codes. Once you have found a publication, search by using the index and table of contents. Westlaw and LexisNexis contain many uniform laws and model codes.

X. Legal Ethics

The conduct of lawyers in Texas is regulated by the *Texas Disciplinary Rules of Professional Conduct*. The rules are based on the A.B.A.'s *Model Rules of Professional Conduct* and cover issues such as the client-lawyer relationship; the lawyer's role as counselor and advocate; limits on a lawyer's transactions with persons who are not clients; and the responsibilities within a law firm of supervising attorneys, junior attorneys, and legal assistants.

These rules are available at the State Bar of Texas website and in the West deskbook *Texas Rules of Court: State*. Very useful commentary on adoption of the rules in Texas is contained in Schuwerk & Sutton, *A Guide to the Texas Disciplinary Rules of Professional Conduct*. Disciplinary opinions concerning Texas attorneys are published in the *Texas Bar Journal* and archived online in the *Texas Ethics Reporter* at the University of Houston's law library website. A very useful looseleaf service on professional ethics is the *ABA/BNA Lawyers' Manual on Professional Conduct*.

XI. Jury Instructions

Before the jury deliberates on the evidence heard during a trial, the judge instructs the jury on the questions of fact they must answer under the legal rules determining the outcome of the trial. The jury instructions thus state the elements of a crime or cause of action and define legal terms. Although the judge determines the applicable law and delivers the instructions to the jury, the instructions are often drafted by counsel for the parties and submitted to the judge for consideration. Lawyers use pattern or model jury instructions as aids for formulating the instructions they submit to the court. Be aware that pattern or model jury instructions cannot cover all possible circumstances and that instructions may need to be drafted specifically for a trial. Researchers might also look to pattern or model jury instructions to see how the courts state the law in the jurisdiction in order to better prepare for the trial.

In some jurisdictions, model jury instructions are drafted by committees appointed by a court, such as the supreme court of the state, and are published after review and approval by the court for use in the courts of the jurisdiction. In Texas, the Committee on Pattern Jury Charges of the State Bar of Texas develops pattern jury instructions, which are published in several volumes, such as *Texas Pattern Jury Charges: Business, Consumer, Insurance, Employment*. In these volumes, each pattern charge is supplemented by comments identifying the legal authority supporting the jury charge and giving suggestions for use. Other sources of jury charges are published privately. Actual charges from trials are reported in *Texas Court's Charge Reporter.*

Jury instructions are published for use in the federal courts by experts in federal practice. A prominent example is O'Malley, Grenig & Lee, *Federal Jury Practice and Instructions.*

Appendix A

Legal Citation

I. Basic Principles

The reader of any legal analysis must be informed of the authority supporting every statement about the law. Statutes, regulations, treaties, judicial opinions, or other primary legal sources must be identified precisely. Statements based on secondary authority must be properly attributed. The reader must be able to confirm all assertions about primary law and ascertain the nature and degree of support provided by all authority. Analysis not properly supported by reference to authority for every statement about the law will not be credible to judges, attorneys, or others who rely upon the research to inform their judgment on legal matters. Legal citation practices provide concise and unique identification for all supporting authority. See Table A-1 for a summary of the purposes of legal citation.

Readers of legal analysis must be able to ascertain immediately the support for every statement about the law. A tremendous variety of resources must be citable in much abbreviated form, with no uncertainty about what is being cited. For this reason, rules dictate every detail of citations. These rules may seem arbitrary. Why is Department abbreviated "Dep't," while Development is abbreviated "Dev."? Why must you use "&" instead of "and" or "§ " instead of "sec."? Some rules have identifiable reasons, while others are simply conventions. The important thing is to learn to apply the rules correctly and consistently. Knowing the citation rules for your jurisdiction and workplace is essential.

Table A-1. Purposes of Legal Citations

1. Show the reader where to find the cited material.
2. Indicate the weight and persuasiveness of each authority. Such information as the court that decided the case, the author of a document, or the publication date of an authority helps the reader assess the authority cited.
3. Convey the type and degree of support the authority lends to the proposition for which it is cited. A citation may, for example, indicate whether the authority supports a point directly or only implicitly.
4. Demonstrate to the reader that your analysis is the result of careful research.

Source: Adapted from *ALWD Citation Manual*

II. State and Local Citation Rules

This appendix is primarily concerned with Texas citation rules. Unlike some other states, Texas does not have a statutorily established set of general citation rules, although the rules of procedure dictate certain citation elements. Texas lawyers and those writing about Texas law follow *The Greenbook: Texas Rules of Form*, commonly known as the *Greenbook*.[1] The *Greenbook* establishes the *Bluebook* as the source of the basic rules of form in Texas: "The *Greenbook* is intended primarily as a supplement to the *Bluebook* to address citation problems unique to Texas; in cases of conflict, the *Greenbook* should be followed in citing Texas authorities."[2] For this reason, this appendix discusses primarily *Bluebook* citation rules and prominent exceptions to those rules required by the *Greenbook*. An alternative citation manual, the *ALWD Citation Manual: A Professional System of Citation* (*ALWD*), now in its fourth edition, will also be discussed.

The *Greenbook*, *Bluebook*, and *ALWD* are not the only citation systems. Some states have rules for citation in practice before their

---

1. The *Greenbook* is produced by the Texas Law Review Association and published under license by the University of Texas at Austin School of Law. The *Greenbook* is in its twelfth edition.
2. Introduction to *Greenbook*, at iv.

courts, courts may establish citation rules in their local rules,[3] and law firms and other organizations may develop their own citation rules. Be sure to know and follow the rules of your jurisdiction and place of work. Once you understand basic citation principles, adapting to different rules is not difficult.

III. Texas Citations under the *Bluebook* and the *Greenbook*

The *Bluebook* was developed by the student editors of four Ivy League law schools. It is now in its nineteenth edition. Since some rules are changed in each edition, it is essential to work with the most current edition of the *Bluebook*. The *Bluebook* is primarily concerned with providing detailed rules for the many questions of citation that arise in the law review publication process. The most useful part of the *Bluebook* for the novice and for most of the questions arising in practice is the relatively brief part called the "Bluepages." The Bluepages are a how-to guide to basic legal citation. While the *Bluebook* typeface rules for law review citations are quite complex, the Bluepages use typeface conventions commonly used in the legal profession. Although the Bluepages provide a useful introduction to legal citation, the detailed rules in the remainder of the *Bluebook* must still be referred to when the simple examples of the Bluepages do not answer a question about citation.

The *Bluebook* requires different typeface conventions for law review citations. Remember to convert any examples from the main body of the *Bluebook* to the practitioner-oriented typefaces of the Bluepages. With the twelfth edition, the *Greenbook* has adopted typographical conventions appropriate for legal documents and memoranda in its examples. *Texas Legal Research* uses the practitioner-oriented typefaces of the Bluepages and the *Greenbook* in its citations.

---

3. Local court rules are listed in *Bluebook* Table BT.2 and *ALWD* Appendix 2.

A. Using the *Bluebook*

The best place to start learning the *Bluebook* rules is in the Bluepages. After these basics are mastered, it will sometimes be necessary to locate specialized citation rules in the rest of the *Bluebook*. A brief table of contents is provided on the back cover, and a more detailed table of contents appears in the front of the book. The very detailed index to the *Bluebook* is often more useful for finding a precise rule. The index indicates pages with instruction on rule application in black type and pages with examples in blue type. Since examples are so useful in learning citation, the *Bluebook* has two pages of common examples for court documents and legal memoranda on the inside of the back cover and its facing page. On the inside of the front cover and its facing page are examples of common citation forms and typeface conventions for law review footnotes. When examples use law review typefaces anywhere in the *Bluebook*, be sure to convert to the Bluepages typeface conventions if you are producing a legal practice document or memorandum.

In addition to rules for forming citations, the *Bluebook* also offers guidance on matters of style, including quotations, italicization and capitalization, and numerals and symbols. Table T.6 specifies abbreviations that must be used for many names and terms. Refer to Table T.6 if you are creating a citation, unless you are absolutely certain of the proper abbreviation. Tables T.1 and T.2 are extremely useful. Table T.1 indicates for the U.S. federal law-making bodies and for each of the states the current and historical publications in which the primary authority for the jurisdiction appears, the years of publication of each source, and the preferred sources for citation where more than one source for a type of authority is available. Table T.2 provides similar information for many foreign countries. These tables also provide some useful background information about the histories of the courts and other institutions.

B. Incorporating Citations into a Document

Legal citations are placed on the same page as the statement they support, rather than in separate tables. Law reviews and law journals

Table A-2. Examples of Citation Sentences and Citation Clauses

Citation Sentences: A robbery is committed if a person recklessly causes bodily injury to another in the course of committing a theft with intent to obtain control of the property of another. Tex. Penal Code § 20.02(a)(1) (West 2003). The term "property" includes anything severed from land. Tex. Penal Code § 29.01(2)(A) (West 2003).

Citation Clauses: Texas statutes define both robbery, Tex. Penal Code § 29.02 (West 2003), and aggravated robbery, Tex. Penal Code § 29.03 (West 2003).

place citations in footnotes. Legal memoranda and court documents place the citations in the text, immediately following the statements they support. If a citation supports an entire sentence, the citation is placed in a separate "citation sentence." BB 4, Rule B2.[4] A citation sentence begins with a capital letter and ends with a period. If a citation supports only part of a sentence, the citation is placed in a "citation clause" immediately following the proposition it supports. BB 4, Rule B2. A citation clause is preceded by a comma and does not begin with a capital letter, unless the citation would otherwise begin with a capital. A citation clause is followed by a comma, unless it is the last clause within a sentence. See Table A-2 for examples of citation sentences and citation clauses.

Remember that citations indicate what primary or secondary legal authority supports a statement. Do not cite your client's facts or your conclusions about the application of a case, statute, or other law to your particular facts. Do not provide a cite for the following statement: "Since ABC Corp. is an affiliate of the debtor and the transfer was within one year of the petition for bankruptcy, the transfer may be avoided." This statement presents facts unique to the situation and

---

4. Throughout this appendix, references will be provided to *Bluebook* (BB), *Greenbook* (GB), and *ALWD Citation Manual* (*ALWD*) pages and rule numbers in this fashion: manual and page number, rule. The rule number is likely to remain the same in subsequent editions of each manual, though the page numbers will probably change.

your conclusions, not a statement of a legal principle found in some authority.

C. Case Citations

1. Essential Components of a Case Citation

Certain information must be included in any case citation. Some information may or may not be present in a particular case citation. The elements that must be contained in a cite for a case published in a reporter are (1) the name of the case; (2) the volume number and abbreviated name of the reporter; (3) the page on which the case begins; (4) the pinpoint cite to the page or pages containing the idea you are citing; (5) the court that decided the case; and (6) the year the case was decided. The elements must appear in the above order. BB 7–13, Rule B4.1.

> EXAMPLE: *Casanova v. Dubois*, 289 F.3d 142, 146 (1st Cir. 2002).

First, the names of the parties on each side are given. If there is more than one party on a side, use only the name of the first party listed. If a party is an individual, give only the party's last name. If a party is a company or other organization, abbreviate the name using the abbreviations in Table T.6. BB 8, Rule B4.1.1. In legal documents or memoranda, underline the entire case name. BB 7, Rule B4.1.1 (Bluepages Tip). You may substitute italic type wherever underlining is used in the *Bluebook*, so long as you are consistent. BB 3, Introduction.

The "v." in the case name is the required abbreviation for the word "versus." Do not use a capital "V." or "vs." The case name must be followed by a comma and a space.

Next is the volume number of the case reporter series, followed by a space and the required abbreviation for the reporter series. You cannot choose how to abbreviate the reporter name; check Table T.1 for the correct abbreviation and the reporter to cite when a case is printed in more than one reporter. When citing Texas cases, refer to the *Greenbook*, which differs from the *Bluebook* in this respect. The *Bluebook* directs that the *South Western Reporter* be cited, if the case is published in it. The *Greenbook* does not require parallel citation to official Texas reporters and *South Western Reporter* in either legal memoranda or court documents, but it provides a citation form to use if local court rules require parallel citations. GB 9, Rule 2.3.2, GB 13, Rule 3.3. (Exception: courts of civil appeals cases 1892 to 1911 must have parallel cites in documents filed with courts. GB 19, Rule 4.2.2.) Following the abbreviated reporter name is a space and the page on which the case begins, followed by a comma, a space, and the pinpoint cite, followed by a space. BB 9, Rule B4.1.2. If the pinpoint cite is the one on which the case begins, repeat the page number. If the pinpoint cite is to a range of pages, give the first and last page of the range, connected by a dash. Repeat only the last two digits (e.g., 528–29).

The parenthetical contains at a minimum the abbreviated name of the court and the date of the decision, separated by a space. BB 10, Rule B4.1.3. The name of the court has only one correct abbreviation; refer to Tables T.1 and T.7 of the *Bluebook* for the proper abbreviation. The *Greenbook* states that citations to opinions of the Texas intermediate courts "must include a reference to the city in which the particular court sits, because one court rule may follow a rule of law different from that followed by another." GB 19, Rule 4.3.1. For example, the parenthetical for a case decided by the Third Court of Appeals, which sits in Austin, would be in the form (Tex. App.—Austin 1985).

The date in the parenthetical for a reported case is the year in which the case was decided. Do not use the date of the petition for review or other procedural date, or the date of the publication of the reporter. Finally, the parenthetical for a case decided in a Texas intermediate court must include a notation showing the disposition of a petition for review or writ of error by the Texas Supreme Court or the Texas Court of Criminal Appeals. GB 20, Rule 4.4., GB 23, Rule 4.5.[5] The complex subject of Texas petition and writ history notation is discussed in Part III.C.4. of this appendix.

You were probably surprised that the directions above indicated the location of every space. Spaces matter. Omitting a space or including a space where none should be is a citation error. A common rule of spacing to watch out for is that when single letters are adja-

---

5. If the Texas Supreme Court or Court of Criminal Appeals has given a reason for granting or refusing a request for review, the disposition is shown as subsequent history rather than petition or writ history notation. GB 26, Rule 4.6.1(b).

Table A-3. Placement of a Full Citation

Assume this is the first time the case is mentioned in the document.

CORRECT: Foreseeability and cause-in-fact are the two elements of proximate cause. *Atchison, Topeka & Santa Fe Ry. Co. v. Cruz,* 9 S.W.3d 173, 178 (Tex. App.—El Paso 1999, pet. granted, judgm't vacated w.r.m.).

CORRECT: In *Atchison, Topeka & Santa Fe Ry. Co. v. Cruz,* 9 S.W.3d 173,
(but should 178 (Tex. App.—El Paso 1999, pet. granted, judgm't vacated
be avoided) w.r.m.), the court noted that foreseeability and cause-in-fact are the two elements of proximate cause.

---

cent, no space is inserted between them, but that if part of an abbreviation is more than one letter there is a space between that part and adjacent parts of the abbreviation. For example, the reporter *Federal Supplement* is abbreviated F. Supp., with a space between the abbreviations. By comparison, the reporter *Federal Rules Decisions* is abbreviated F.R.D., with no spaces. When you use an abbreviation found in a table in the *Bluebook,* note carefully where spaces occur and use that exact form in your citation.

2. Full and Short Citations to Cases

The first time a case is cited in a document, use the full citation, with all the elements discussed above. To make it easier for the reader to understand the substance of a sentence requiring a citation, it is best to place a full citation after the proposition for which it is cited. Although it is not technically wrong, placing a full citation at the start of a sentence makes the sentence more difficult to read. See Table A-3 for an example of how the location of a cite affects readability.

Once a full citation has been used, a short form can be used for subsequent cites to the same authority. BB 13, Rule B4.2. Short form citations can take several forms. The important thing is that the short form give enough information to make clear which earlier, full citation is referred to, the full form and short form appear in the same general discourse, and the citation is easy to locate. BB 13, Rule B4.2.

A good practice is to include the name of one of the parties, most commonly the first party, in the short form. All short form citations should include a pinpoint, preceded by "at."

Id. is used to refer to the authority in the immediately preceding citation. When *id.* is not the first word in a sentence, it is not capitalized. *Id.* alone refers to the exact pinpoint in the preceding cite. If citing to the same authority, but a different page, use "*id.* at [new page number]," as in "*id.* at 8." Only use *id.* when the preceding cite refers to only one authority. The *Bluebook* has additional rules for the use of *id.* See Rule B4.2 for a summary of the most important usage rules and Rule 10.9 for more detailed instructions.

3. Prior and Subsequent History

A case may result in several published opinions in the course of litigation. *Bluebook* Rule B4.1.6 requires that a full case citation usually must include "subsequent history," showing the opinions later in the course of litigation of the case cited. Certain exceptions to the requirement for subsequent history are listed in Rule 10.7. A major exception is that denials of discretionary appeals, such as certiorari, are not included unless the denial occurred with the last two years or the denial is particularly relevant. BB 101, Rule 10.7. Texas citation practice is a major exception to *Bluebook* Rule 10.7. As discussed in Chapter 4, Part XII., the disposition of any application for review on appeal must be noted in a cite. See Part C.4. of this section for discussion of *Greenbook* rules for citation of appeals from Texas intermediate courts.

Prior history is usually not included, but may be when it has particular significance for the statement supported by the cite or where the case cited is not itself informative, as in memorandum opinions by the U.S. Supreme Court. BB 101, Rule 10.7. If prior history is included, it is given before the subsequent history. BB 102, Rule 10.7.1.

EXAMPLE: *Kubrick v. United States*, 581 F.2d 1092 (3d Cir. 1978), *aff'g* 435 F. Supp. 166 (E.D. Pa. 1977), *rev'd*, 444 U.S. 111 (1979).[6]

---

6. Example from *Bluebook*, at 102.

Table A-4. Writ History Notation (Before September 1, 1997)

Abbreviation	Meaning
1. writ ref'd	1. Writ refused.
2. writ ref'd n.r.e.	2. Writ refused, no reversible error.
3. writ denied	3. Writ denied.
4. no writ	4. No writ.
5. writ dism'd by agr.	5. Writ dismissed by agreement.
6. writ dism'd	6. Writ dismissed.
7. writ dism'd w.o.j.	7. Writ dismissed for want of jurisdiction.
8. writ dism'd judgm't cor.	8. Writ dismissed, judgment correct.
9. writ ref'd w.o.m.	9. Writ refused for want of merit.
10. writ granted w.r.m.	10. Writ granted without reference to merits.
11. writ granted	11. Writ granted.

4. Texas Writ and Petition History

The Texas Supreme Court and Texas Court of Criminal Appeals consider whether to review a case when an application is filed requesting review. A cite to any case from an intermediate court must show the disposition of the case by the Texas Supreme Court or the Texas Court of Criminal Appeals. GB 20, Rule 4.4; GB 23, Rule 4.5. The notation required depends on whether the case is civil or criminal.

a. Civil Cases

Before September 1, 1997, a "writ of error" was filed with the Texas Supreme Court for review of a case decided by a Texas court of appeals or a Texas court of civil appeals. The "writ history" is indicated in the citation by including in the court parenthetical one of several notations. GB 23, Rule 4.4.2. The notations for writ of error dispositions are listed in Table A-4.

> EXAMPLE: *Bd. of Adjustment v. Rich*, 328 S.W. 2d 798 (Tex. Civ. App.—Fort Worth 1959, writ ref'd).[7]

---

7. Example from *Greenbook*, at 14.

The precedential weight of a case depends on the writ history notation. The highest precedential weight is "writ ref'd" (writ refused), meaning the Texas Supreme Court agrees with the judgment and reasoning of the court of appeals or the court of civil appeals. Cases with the notation "writ ref'd" have precedential weight equal to opinions of the Texas Supreme Court. The precedential value of some other notations depends on whether review was obligatory or discretionary at the time of the appeal.[8] Review of a writ of error was obligatory from September 1, 1892, through June 30, 1917, and from June 14, 1927, through June 19, 1987. At all other times, review has been in the discretion of the Texas Supreme Court. The meanings of particular notations are explained in Appendix E of the *Greenbook*. Appendix E also gives the time periods during which particular notations were used.

An application filed with the Texas Supreme Court on or after September 1, 1997, to review a case decided by a Texas court of appeals is called a "petition for review." Any disposition of a petition for review must be included in a cite for a court of appeals case in the court parenthetical. GB 20–22, Rule 4.4. The notations for civil case petitions for review are listed in Table A-5. A common source of confusion is the difference between "no pet. h." and "no pet." The notation "no pet. h." means no petition has been filed, but the time for filing has not yet expired. The notation "no pet." means the time for filing has passed and no petition was filed.

EXAMPLE: *Farmer v. Holley*, 237 S.W.3d 758 (Tex. App.—
Waco 2007, pet. denied).

Review of petitions for review is within the discretion of the Texas Supreme Court. Nonetheless, an opinion with the notation "pet. ref'd" (petition refused) has the same precedential value as an opinion of the Texas Supreme Court.[9] Otherwise, notations for denials

---

8. A thorough study of the history and the weight of the various notations is provided in Dylan O. Drummond, *Citation Writ Large*, 20 App. Advoc. 89 (2008).

9. Tex. R. App. P. § 56.1(c) (West 2007). Texas practice is unique in this respect. In other jurisdictions, refusal by an appellate court to review a case on discretionary appeal has no precedential value.

Table A-5. Petition for Review History Notation
(On or after September 1, 1997)

Abbreviation	Meaning
1. pet. ref'd	1. Petition refused.
2. pet. denied	2. Petition denied.
3. no pet. h,.	3. No petition history.
4. no pet.	4. No petition.
5. pet. filed	5. Petition filed.
6. pet. dism'd by agr.	6. Petition dismissed by agreement of the parties.
7. pet. withdrawn	7. Petition withdrawn.
8. pet. dism'd w.o.j.	8. Petition dismissed for want of jurisdiction.
9. pet. struck	9. Petition struck.
10. pet. dism'd	10. Petition dismissed.
11. pet. granted, judgm't vacated w.r.m.	11. Petition granted, judgment vacated without reference to the merits.
12. pet. granted	12. Petition granted.
13. pet. abated	13. Petition abated.

and dismissals of petitions for review do not indicate the decision of the court concerning the merits of the lower court's opinion.[10] Appendix D of the *Greenbook* provides notation meanings, weight, and the defining rule of appellate procedure (for certain notations).

b. Criminal Cases

A citation of a criminal case decided by a Texas court of appeals must include in the court parenthetical a notation of the disposition of the "petition for review" filed with the Texas Court of Criminal Appeals. GB 23, Rule 4.5.[11] The petition history in crim-

---

10. *Loram Maint. of Way, Inc. v. Ianni*, 210 S.W.3d 593, 596 (Tex. 2006).

11. If the Texas Court of Criminal Appeals has given a reason for granting or refusing a request for review, the disposition is shown as subsequent history, rather than as petition notation. GB 26, Rule 4.6.1(b).

Table A-6. Petition History Notation in Criminal Cases

Abbreviation	Meaning
1. no pet. h.	1. No petition history.
2. no pet.	2. No petition.
3. pet. filed	3. Petition filed.
4. pet. dism'd	4. Petition dismissed.
5. pet. ref'd, untimely filed	5. Petition refused, untimely filed.
6. pet. ref'd	6. Petition refused.
7. pet. granted	7. Petition granted.
8. rev. granted, without pet.	8. Review granted, without petition.

inal cases does not affect the precedential weight of the case.[12] The notations are listed in Table A-6.

See Chapter 4, Part XII., for additional discussion of the precedential value of writ and petition notations.

c. Exceptions to Noting Writ and Petition History in the Court Parenthetical

Exceptions to the rule that petition or writ history is included as a notation within the court parenthetical apply when the Texas Supreme Court or Texas Court of Criminal Appeals publishes an opinion explaining the action on a petition or writ, or for any disposition after granting a writ or petition. In those instances, the opinion is treated as subsequent history in the full citation. GB 22, Rule 4.4; GB 24, Rule 4.5; GB 26, Rule 4.6.1(b).

EXAMPLE: *Weaver v. Westchester Fire Ins. Co.*, 730 S.W.2d 834 (Tex. App.—Waco), *writ ref'd*, 739 S.W.2d 23 (Tex. 1987) (per curiam).

EXAMPLE: *RepublicBank Dallas, N.A. v. Interkal, Inc.*, 677 S.W.2d 759 (Tex. App.—Dallas 1984), *rev'd on other grounds*, 691 S.W.2d 605 (Tex. 1985).[13]

---

12. *Oldham v. State*, 977 S.W.2d 569, 570 (Tex. Crim. App. 1996) (citing numerous opinions by the court).

13. Examples from *Greenbook,* at 26.

D. Signals

Introductory signals, such as *see* or *e.g.*, are used to indicate the level of support an authority provides for a statement. For example, *see* is used to introduce authority supporting, but not directly stating, the proposition for which it is cited. BB 5–6, Rule B3.3. The signal *e.g.*, is used to introduce one of multiple authorities that could be cited as directly stating a proposition. BB 6, Rule B3.2. *See* and *e.g.*, can be combined as *see, e.g.*, to introduce an authority as one of multiple authorities supporting, but not directly stating, a proposition. Other signals and their uses are explained at BB 54–56, Rule 1.2.

E. Explanatory Parentheticals

Additional information can be added to a cite in one or more parentheticals following the court and date parenthetical. Explanatory parentheticals may include indicators of weight of authority, such as *per curiam* or *en banc*. They may give the names of judges issuing concurring or dissenting opinion. They are often used to give brief quotes from the authority or brief explanations about the authority. BB 12, Rule B4.1.5 and BB 59–60, Rule 1.5.

F. Quotations

Quotations should generally be used sparingly. If you have absorbed and synthesized the material you will be able to write the ideas in your own words. Quotations are best used in situations where reproducing the exact wording of authority is critical, such as quoting to a court the exact language of a statute.

Most quotes will be relatively short and included within the body of the text of the document. The *Bluebook* states that quotes of fifty or more words should be in indented blocks of text, with no quotation marks. BB 76, Rule 5.1. When quoting, be sure everything is copied exactly, including punctuation, italics, and capitals. Indicate if anything is omitted or changed. Do not correct misspellings or misstatements in a quote; indicate you are aware of the error with "[sic]." Remember to place commas and periods within quotes and all other punctuation outside the quotation marks. *Bluebook* Rule 5 gives detailed instructions on use and formatting of quotes. BB 76–79, Rule 5.

G. Common Citation Problems

1. Federal Statutes

Federal statutes are published in the official publication, *United States Code* (U.S.C.). When citing statutes, the U.S.C. should be cited whenever possible. BB 114, Rule 12.3. However, public laws are included in the U.S.C. only after a considerable delay. The commercially published *United States Code Annotated* (U.S.C.A.) and *United States Code Service* (U.S.C.S.) are kept current and are usually used for research. If the most recent updates of a statute have been included in the U.S.C., use that, but be careful in citing. Many novices will give a U.S.C. cite, but give the current year for the date. Since the U.S.C. is only published every six years, with annual supplements, this usually indicates the person citing did not actually refer to the U.S.C. If you cite the U.S.C., use the date of the volume or volumes in which the current language of the statute is found.

If you cite the U.S.C.A. or the U.S.C.S. versions, cite the publication date of the main volume, if it contains the current statutory language; cite the main volume and the most current supplement (usually the pocket part), if both must be referred to; and cite just the supplement if the current statutory language appears only there. BB 114–115, Rules 12.3, 12.3.1. Even if you have used the U.S.C.A. on Westlaw or the U.S.C.S. on LexisNexis to find the current statutory language, you must cite the print versions. A common mistake in citing the U.S.C.A. or U.S.C.S. is to use the current date, since the online versions show that they are current to within a week or two of the time of viewing.

EXAMPLE: (Statutory language appears in both the bound volume and a supplemental volume of the *United States Code*): 11 U.S.C. § 101(4A) (2000 & Supp. V 2005).

EXAMPLE: (Statutory language appears in both the bound volume and the supplement of West's *United States Code Annotated*): 11 U.S.C.A. § 101(4A) (West 2004 & Supp. 2008).

EXAMPLE: (Statutory language appears in just the main volume of West's *United States Code Annotated*): 12 U.S.C.A. § 21 (West 2001).

EXAMPLE: (Statutory language appears in just the supplement): 42 U.S.C.A. § 1395dd (West Supp. 2007).

2. Abbreviations

When formulating citations, check the *Bluebook* tables for required abbreviations for case names, court names, months, and reporter names. If a table does not include a specific word, see the general instructions for abbreviation at the beginning of the table. Do not abbreviate words in the text of a memo or court document. A special application of the rule that words not be abbreviated in the text is that ordinals ending in two or three end in "2nd" or "3rd" in text, although they are abbreviated as "2d" or "3d" in citations. BB 82, Rule 6.2(b)(ii).

3. Spaces

Observe carefully the rules for placement of spaces. Within an abbreviation, remember that if one part of an abbreviation has more than one letter, there is a space between it and the parts of the abbreviation on either side. There is no space between single letters. For example, there is no space in the abbreviation "L.J." for Law Journal, while "L. Rev." for Law Review has a space. BB 80, Rule 6.1. For purposes of this spacing rule, ordinal abbreviations such as "2d" or "3d", are treated as one letter, as in "S.W.2d".

4. Numbers

The general rule is to spell out numbers from zero to ninety-nine and to use numerals for larger numbers. If a number begins a sentence, however, spell it out. Round numbers (such as "hundred" or "thousand") may be spelled out, if done consistently. BB 81, Rule 6.2(a).

5. Use of the Procedural Phrases In re and Ex rel.

In case names, use *In re* as the abbreviation for "in the matter of," "petition of," "application of," and similar procedural expressions. Use *Ex rel.* for "on the relation of," "on behalf of," "as next friend of," and similar expressions. Italicize all procedural phrases. BB 8, Rule B.4.1.1(iv) and BB 90, Rule 10.2.1(b).

H. Using the *Bluebook* for Law Review Citation

This appendix has emphasized Bluepages citation practices, used by practitioners in writing legal memoranda and court documents. While cites in practitioner memoranda and documents are placed in the body of the text, citations in law reviews and law journals are placed in footnotes at the bottom of the page. The many examples in the main pages of the *Bluebook* are in the typeface conventions the *Bluebook* requires for footnotes. This makes the *Bluebook* examples easier to apply for writers and editors of journals.

The *Bluebook* uses ordinary type, italics, and large and small capital letters for citation in footnotes. Table A-7 shows the use of the three typefaces commonly used in law review footnotes. Some law reviews may use only ordinary type and italics, or just ordinary type. BB 62–63, Rule 2.1. A convenient reminder of when to use the three typefaces is provided by the Quick Reference: Law Review Footnotes, on the back of the front cover and its facing page at the beginning of the *Bluebook*.

A case name in a footnote is printed in plain type, while a case name in the body of the text is italicized. BB 64, Rule 2.2. Refer to Rule 2 for the typeface to use in footnotes and in the text for each type of authority.

Table A-7. *Bluebook* Typefaces for Law Review Footnotes

Typeface Used	Example
Use ordinary type for case names in full citations.	Lochner v. New York, 198 U.S. 45 (1905).
Use italics for the short form of case citations.	*Lochner*, 198 U.S. at 50.
For books, use large and small capital letters for the author and the title.	RICHARD KLUGER, SIMPLE JUSTICE (1976).
For articles, use ordinary type for the author's name, italics for the article title, and large and small capitals for the periodical title. If a case name appears in an article title, use ordinary type.	Cass R. Sunstein, Lochner's Legacy, 87 COLUM. L. REV. 873 (1987).
Use italics for all explanatory phrases, such as *aff'g*, *cert. denied*, and *overruled by*.	Oreck Corp. v. Whirlpool Corp., 579 F.2d 126, 131 (2d Cir. 1978) (en banc), *cert. denied*, 439 U.S. 946 (1978).
Use italics for all introductory signals, such as *see* and *e.g.* when they appear in citations, as opposed to text.	*See, e.g.*, Parker Drilling Co. v. Ferguson, 391 F.2d 581 (5th Cir. 1968).

The rules of use for short cites in footnotes are generally the same as the rules discussed in this appendix for short cites in the text of practitioner documents.

IV. *ALWD Citation Manual*

The *ALWD Citation Manual* (*ALWD*), now in its fourth edition, was first published in 2000 by the Association of Legal Writing Directors. The purpose of *ALWD* is to provide a citation manual that is easier to use and learn from than is the *Bluebook*. Unlike the *Bluebook*, the *ALWD* uses the same system of typefaces for cites in law review articles and for practitioner documents. The use of the same typefaces for all purposes eliminates the need to convert examples in law review typefaces to the typefaces used in practitioner documents, a troublesome feature of the *Bluebook*. The *ALWD* manual has made other changes intended to simplify and make more consistent citation practices, resulting in some differences between *ALWD* and *Bluebook* rules.

A. Using the *ALWD Citation Manual*

Before using the *ALWD* manual, read "How to Use This Book," in Part I.B. on pages 4–7. This part explains the overall organization of the book and the organization within each part of the book and gives additional tips about use of the manual. The manual provides two finding tools: the table of contents and the index. The table of contents aids understanding of the manual and helps in locating parts dealing with major sources of law. The index is very detailed and best used to locate answers to specific citation questions. The manual contains many examples, including "Fast Formats" showing common examples of citations for each type of authority. Examples are often easier to understand than abstract statements of the rules. Appendices provide guides to sources for state and federal jurisdictions, local court citation rules, abbreviations, and a guide to federal tax materials. A useful feature for the law student is Appendix 6, an example of a legal memorandum.

As with the *Bluebook*, changes are made to the *ALWD* manual with each edition. Be sure to use most current edition of whatever citation manual you are using.

B. Differences between the *ALWD Citation Manual* and the *Bluebook*

Besides eliminating the distinction between law review and practitioner typefaces, *ALWD* rules differ in some other respects from *Bluebook* rules.

The list of general abbreviations in Appendix 3 has many more abbreviations than does Table T.6 in the *Bluebook*. Further, the *ALWD Manual* provides options for some abbreviations. For example, the *Bluebook* abbreviates "Department" as "Dep't," while *ALWD* recognizes either "Dep't" or "Dept." as acceptable abbreviations.

The *Bluebook* requires that "United States" never be abbreviated when it is a party's name in a case name. BB 94–95, Rule 10.2.2. *ALWD* allows use of either "U.S." or "United States." ALWD 78, 12.2(g).

The rule for quotations is slightly different in *ALWD*. While the *Bluebook* requires that quotes of fifty words or more be in an indented block, *ALWD* requires indented blocks where a quote is either fifty or more words or spans more than four lines of text. ALWD 390, 47.5(a).

The researcher who has been trained in the *Bluebook* will not find it difficult to convert to use of *ALWD* citation rules. Aside from typeface conventions, the major rules are the same in both manuals. Awareness of the relatively few systematic differences, together with regular reference to the manual as citations are formed, is the key to moving successfully from one citation system to another.

V. Editing Citations

While you are researching and writing, be sure to record all the information you will need for proper citation. Try to record the information in proper citation form in your research journal at the time you are using a resource. When you write your final work product, double check all cites for proper citation form and substantive accuracy. Look again at the original source to confirm that it actually supports the proposition for which it is being cited. It is quite possible that your perspective on the meaning and significance of the source will have evolved since you originally encountered it in your research.

As you edit your drafts, the placement and relationship of cites to each other may change. Rather than use "*id.*" cites in initial drafts, use short forms for cites and replace them with "*id.*" only when the draft is in final form. If you are writing for publication where footnotes or endnotes are used, be sure to recheck all cross-references before submitting. As footnotes are added, deleted, or moved during the rewriting process, cross-references need to be adjusted.

Checking and correcting citations can be very time consuming. Allow time for citation editing in your project plan. Your analysis will be more credible if not marred by errors in citation.

Appendix B

Selected Bibliography

General Research (tending to focus on federal material)

Steven M. Barkan et al., *Fundamentals of Legal Research* (9th ed., Found. Press 2009).

Robert C. Berring & Elizabeth A. Edinger, *Finding the Law* (12th ed., West 2005).

Morris L. Cohen & Kent C. Olson, *Legal Research in a Nutshell* (9th ed., West 2007).

Christina L. Kunz et al., *The Process of Legal Research* (7th ed., Aspen Publishers 2008).

Amy E. Sloan, *Basic Legal Research: Tools and Strategies* (4th ed., Aspen Publishers 2009).

Texas Research

Lydia M.V. Brandt, *Texas Legal Research: An Essential Lawyering Skill* (Tex. Lawyer Press 1995).

Matthew C. Cordon & Brandon D. Quarles, *Specialized Topics in Texas Legal Research* (Hein 2005).

Janice C. May, *The Texas State Constitution: A Reference Guide* (Greenwood Press 1996). Reprinted as *The Texas State Constitution* (Oxford University Press 2011).

Brandon D. Quarles & Matthew C. Cordon, *Researching Texas Law* (2d ed., Hein 2008).

Advanced Legal Research

J.D.S. Armstrong & Christopher A. Knott, *Where the Law Is: An Introduction to Advanced Legal Research* (3d ed., West 2009).

Specialized Research

Specialized Legal Research (Penny A. Hazelton, ed., Aspen Publishers Supp. 2011) (formerly edited by Leah F. Chanin).

Nancy P. Johnson, *Sources of Compiled Legislative Histories: A Bibliography of Government Documents, Periodical Articles, and Books* (Rothman 2007).

William A. Raabe et al., *Federal Tax Research* (8th ed., Thomson/South-Western 2009).

Bernard D. Reams, Jr., *Federal Legislative Histories: An Annotated Bibliography and Index to Officially Published Sources* (Greenwood Press 1994).

Legal Analysis

Charles R. Calleros, *Legal Method and Writing* (5th ed., Aspen Publishers 2006).

Bradley G. Clary & Pamela Lysaght, *Successful Legal Analysis and Writing: The Fundamentals* (3d ed., West 2010).

Christine Coughlin, Joan Malmud & Sandy Patrick, *A Lawyer Writes: A Practical Guide to Legal Analysis* (Carolina Academic Press 2008).

Linda H. Edwards, *Legal Writing: Process, Analysis, and Organization* (5th ed., Aspen Publishers 2010).

Linda H. Edwards, *Legal Writing and Analysis* (3d ed., Aspen Publishers 2011).

Michael D. Murray & Christy Hallam DeSanctis, *Legal Research and Writing Across the Curriculum: Problems and Exercises* (Found. Press 2009).

Richard K. Neumann, Jr., *Legal Reasoning and Legal Writing: Structure, Strategy, and Style* (6th ed., Aspen Publishers 2009).

Laurel Currie Oates & Anne Enquist, *The Legal Writing Handbook: Analysis, Research, and Writing* (5th ed., Aspen Publishers 2010).

Jill J. Ramsfield, *Culture to Culture: A Guide to U.S. Legal Writing* (Carolina Academic Press 2005).

Mary Barnard Ray & Barbara J. Cox, *Beyond the Basics: A Text for Advanced Legal Writing* (2d ed., West 2003).

David S. Romantz & Kathleen Elliott Vinson, *Legal Analysis: The Fundamental Skill* (2d ed., Carolina Academic Press 2009).

Deborah A. Schmedemann & Christina L. Kunz, *Synthesis: Legal Reading, Reasoning, and Writing* (3d ed., Aspen Publishers 2007).

Nancy L. Schultz & Louis J. Sirico, Jr., *Legal Writing and Other Lawyering Skills* (5th ed., Aspen Publishers 2010).

Helene S. Shapo, Marilyn R. Walter & Elizabeth Fajans, *Writing and Analysis in the Law* (5th ed., Found. Press 2008).

About the Author

Spencer L. Simons is Director of the O'Quinn Law Library and Associate Professor of Law at the University of Houston Law Center. He holds both a J.D. and an M.B.A. as well as a Master of Librarianship from the University of Washington.

Index

Regulations, *See* Administrative
agencies; Rules and regula-
tions, administrative agen-
cies.
Regulations.gov, 171
Reporters
Agency decisions, 152–153,
186
Federal court opinions, 48,
60–61, 62, 82, 200
Generally, 47–48, 89, 163,
166, 184, 198, 208
Regional, 48–49, 80, 81–82
Specialized, 61, 190, 191
Texas court opinions, 41, 48,
50, 51, 52–57, 59–60, 113,
166, 198–199
Republic of Texas, 33–34, 36,
52–53
Research journal, 10, 11–12, 29,
31, 132, 212
Research process
Administrative law, *See* Ad-
ministrative law.
Bill tracking, *See* Bill tracking.
Constitution, *See* Constitu-
tional law research.
Digests, *See* Digests.
Generally, 6–12
Legislative history, *See* Leg-
islative history research.
Online legal research, *See*
Online legal research.
Secondary sources, *See* Sec-
ondary sources.
Statutes, *See* Statutes.

Unfamiliar areas of law, 4–5,
6–10, 57–58, 173–191
Updating in print, *See* Up-
dating.
Updating online, *See* Updat-
ing.
Research strategy, 10–11
Research terms, *See* Search
terms, generation of.
Restatements, 187–188
Revised Texas Civil Statutes (Revised Civil Statutes), 96,
98–99, 100, 104, 105, 109,
117, 118, 119, 123, 131, 132
Revised Texas Statutes of 1925,
96–97
Rule making
Administrative, 126, 140,
142–145, 148, 155, 171
Court rules, *See* Court rules.
Rules and regulations, administrative agencies
Federal regulations, 148–153,
156, 168–169
Generally, 4, 5, 9, 10, 12, 17,
27, 47, 88, 140, 155, 156,
163, 168–169, 170, 173,
176, 184, 186, 193
Texas administrative rules,
121, 140–146, 176

Scope notes, databases, 16–17,
29, 106–107, 135, 169
Search engines, 22–23, 119
Search terms, generation of
Generally, 3–4, 6–8
Journalistic approach, 7